Blackness and Modernism

Blackness
and Modernism
The Literary Career of John Edgar Wideman

James W. Coleman

University Press of Mississippi
JACKSON AND LONDON

University Press of Mississippi thanks John Edgar Wideman and
the following publishers for granting permission to quote from
the works of John Edgar Wideman.

From *A Glance Away.* Copyright © 1967 by John Edgar Wideman. Reprinted by permission of Harcourt Brace Jovanovich,
Inc.

From *Hiding Place*, copyright © 1981, from *Damballah*, copyright © 1981, and from *Sent for You Yesterday*, copyright ©
1983 by John Edgar Wideman. Reprinted by permission of Random House, Inc.

From *Reuben* by John Edgar Wideman. Copyright © 1987 by
John Edgar Wideman. Reprinted by permission of Henry Holt &
Co., Inc.

The paper in this book meets the guidelines for permanence and
durability of the Committee on Production Guidelines for Book
Longevity of the Council on Library Resources.

Library of Congress Cataloging-in-Publication Data

Coleman, James William, 1947–
    Blackness and modernism : the literary career of John
Edgar Wideman / James W. Coleman.
        p.   cm.
    Bibliography: p.
    Includes index.
    ISBN 0-87805-391-3
    1. Wideman, John Edgar—Criticism and interpretation.
2. Afro-Americans in literature.   3. Modernism (Literature)—
United States.
    I. Title.
PS3573.J26Z6   1989   88-36906
813'.54—dc19   CIP

British Library Cataloguing-in-Publication data is available.

For my parents,
Lucy J. Coleman and the late James H. Coleman,
who encouraged and supported me,
and the late George E. Kent, who guided me.

Contents

Acknowledgments

I thank Joan Cooper, Mary Roth, and Betty Welch, secretaries in the Humanities Division Office at Colorado College, for their hard work in typing my manuscript and for their generosity and kindness, which went beyond the requirements of their jobs. I also express my appreciation to the Colorado College English Department, and particularly to George Butte, chairman, for its support while I was working on this project, and I thank the Colorado College administration, especially Dean David Finley, for its encouragement and monetary support.

To Seetha Srinivasan of the University Press of Mississippi, I express my deep gratitude; from start to finish, her cooperation and help have made this project possible. I salute Keith Byerman and Craig Werner, who read the manuscript, for their comments and criticisms, which allowed me to focus my ideas and develop my argument. I also thank Marcia Brubeck, editor.

James W. Coleman

Blackness and Modernism

Introduction

During his career as a writer-intellectual, John Edgar Wideman in his personal life has overcome feelings of alienation from the black community and has reoriented himself as a participant in black culture. In his fiction, I contend, Wideman has effected a similar shift, using modernism and postmodernism to bring his intellectual characters out of their isolation and into contact with the needs, concerns, and traditions of black people generally. Before he could write about this shift, Wideman had to inform himself about black culture. An eight-year period of immersion in the works of nineteenth- and twentieth-century authors gave him the resources he needed. Using them, he was able to circumvent modernism's dead-end, pessimistic worldview and at the same time to chart a new course for other, similarly estranged black intellectuals.

I identify three main stages in Wideman's career: the early books

(*A Glance Away*, 1967; *Hurry Home*, 1970; and *The Lynchers*, 1973); the Homewood trilogy (*Hiding Place*, 1981; *Damballah*, 1981; and *Sent for You Yesterday*, 1983); and the recent books (*Brothers and Keepers*, 1984; and *Reuben*, 1987).

The early books certainly exhibit differences, but most evident at this point in Wideman's career is his depiction of the black intellectual's isolation from the black community. Wideman was influenced both by the modernist literary treatment of such alienation and, as the circumstances of his life indicate, by his own doubts about the black community and his relationship to it. In his books the black community expresses hostility toward the black intellectual, has interests and concerns that differ from his, and is at times oblivious to him.

In the early books a progression is evident. *A Glance Away* focuses on the mainstream modernist world of white writers and on a modernist white intellectual character who is alienated and isolated from both the white and the black communities. *Hurry Home* shows a black intellectual alienated from the black community and pursuing an existence that the character considers necessary as a means of coping with the hostility of the black community. In *The Lynchers*, black intellectuals attempt to lead and to liberate the black community, but their actions merely isolate and alienate them further from it, so that they exert no impact. It is noteworthy, however, that *Lynchers'* characters do attempt to approach the community, although their efforts fail.

The Homewood trilogy, which followed Wideman's long period of discovery of and immersion in the work of black writers, shows the black intellectual in a meaningful relationship with the black community and integrates modernism and postmodernism with black traditions by means of a black literary voice. In *Hiding Place* the black intellectual's rapprochement with the black community is tentative, but in *Damballah*, the intellectual characters, often obviously surrogates for Wideman himself, feel impelled to understand their alienation from the community and seek to learn and use its oral rituals. The intellectual in *Sent for You Yesterday* maintains a close relationship with blacks while he constructs the fictions and myth that will allow him to function as a helpful, saving force in the community.

Brothers, Wideman's biographical-autobiographical work, provides the transition that truly releases the black intellectual to pursue the personal, subjective life of the intellectual as he strives to serve his people. In *Brothers*, Wideman the writer-intellectual reintegrates himself into the black family and community, and *Reuben* shows that he has finally established his allegiance and his role as an intellectual. His intellectual interests are those of the community, which he is obligated to help as much as he can. He no longer feels obliged to work through a dead-end, pessimistic modernism, and he no longer experiences anxiety about experimenting as a writer: experimentation that serves the goal of the intellectual is acceptable.

In *Reuben*, a black intellectual prepares himself to help the black community. Reuben, a very bookish individual, perceives that postmodernism is well suited to his purposes (and by implication better suited than modernism). He realizes that all perspectives on life are fictions to a significant extent but views postmodernism as helpful because it can easily be manipulated to create helpful fictions that will counteract the harmful ones perpetrated against blacks by white society.

According to postmodernist thinking, the essence of reality is undefinable and unknowable because people have fragmented, disjointed minds and personalities incapable of logical, rational connections. As a result, "fictions" are only arbitrary appropriations of language that do not define reality. The linguistic constructions of T. S. Eliot's modernist poem *The Waste Land*, for example, represent nothing but the subjective expressions of their creator. Eliot's poem is, in effect, not a public statement of cultural reality but merely the private complaint that Eliot once called it. Thus reduced in status, the poem cannot challenge people to reform a cultural reality, and readers cannot even penetrate Eliot's language to discover his subjective feelings; they can know only their own subjective responses, the fictions they create from Eliot's fictions.

Art is silent regarding its own interpretation; the meaning of any literary work is inferred by its readers. A literary work opens itself to different subjective readings; in its interaction with the reader, a literary work is free to "fulfill *itself*. . . , free to catch at the manifold—the atoms as they fall—and create significant harmony not in the universe but within itself. . . . The world, reality, is discontinuous till art comes along. . . , but within art all becomes vital, discontinuous, yes, but within an aesthetic system of positioning" (Bradbury and McFarlane 1976:25). As Wallace Stevens said, the poet (or the writer) cooperates by not pretending to capture reality: he gives reality "the substance and meaning of a fiction"

(Bradbury and McFarlane 1976:25). The artist does not pretend to speak on the "poverty in the universe and a trauma in man" (ibid.), although these things could possibly exist, as Eliot remarked. The artist must take his art to a higher level above reality, to a level where it can fulfill itself and allow readers to fulfill themselves through subjective fictions. At this level alone can it attain authenticity. The artist thus transcends "both history and reality by the dispositions of his technique" (Bradbury and McFarlane 1976:25–26). Postmodernism is both more pessimistic and more optimistic than modernism: it is more pessimistic because it views art as having no ability to change reality; it is more optimistic because it sees an opportunity for subjective fulfillment of the reader and self-fulfillment in art.

In this book I contend that John Edgar Wideman during his career as a novelist has moved from an uncritical acceptance of the forms and themes of mainstream modernism as practiced by white literary masters to a black voicing of modernism and postmodernism that is consistent with Afro-American perspectives and reflects a commitment to the needs of the black community. A number of contemporary black writers have achieved this black voicing; Wideman's comprehension of their achievement, which came during the period of reading and discovery between publication of *Lynchers* and *Hiding Place*, was important in his transition. Wideman shares with such writers as Jean Toomer, Ralph Ellison, James Baldwin, Toni Morrison, Alice Walker, Ishmael Reed, Gayl Jones, William Melvin Kelley, and Leon Forrest the concern with speaking in a modernist and postmodernist literary voice that is black and exhibits a commitment to blackness. The problem confronting all of these writers, including Wideman, is how to bridge the gap between the black community and the modernism and postmodernism of the literary mainstream.

It is hardly unusual for writers or intellectuals to have difficulty in forging a relationship with the community when the culture in question lies outside the mainstream, because success and acceptance in the mainstream depend upon literacy defined in mainstream terms (in this case, proficiency in modernist and postmodernist forms and approaches). Wideman and other twentieth-century black writers have had to find ways to improvise and transform mainstream literacy into one which reflects Afro-American perspectives and approaches. In *From Behind the Veil: A Study of Afro-American Narrative* (1979), Robert B. Stepto talks about Ellison's protagonist in *Invisible Man*, and by implication about Ellison himself, as having achieved such an Afro-American literacy. At the end of the book, the Invisible Man is able to distinguish between "embracing the music [he hears] and making the music [he hears his] own" (Stepto 1979:194). Several of the black figures in Ellison's book are remarkable, not because they "make art out of chaos or out of nothingness, but because they make art out of art." (Stepto 1979:194). To shape their own black voices, and to achieve a literacy that will give them relevance in both mainstream and Afro-American culture, Wideman and other twentieth-century black writers improvise on mainstream art to make their own art "out of art."

Wideman's early books focus on the alienation of the black intellectual from the black community. In these books, Wideman fails to achieve the black voice that will allow him to use modernism, which is the key to his acceptance as part of the mainstream, as a medium for the articulation of Afro-American concerns and responses to life. *Hurry Home* pays the greatest attention to the alienation of the black intellectual; *Lynchers* demonstrates the incipient development of a black literary voice. *Hiding Place* and *Damballah*, the first two books in the Homewood trilogy, use black speech, cultural rituals, and religious songs to express the attitudes and responses that have allowed blacks to rise above oppression and hardship and to flourish spiritually in America. In *Yesterday* Wideman begins to voice postmodernism in a way that suits the needs of the black intellectual and the black community. *Hiding Place* shows the black intellectual moving in only a very tentative way toward the black community, but in *Yesterday*, the intellectual has established the basis for a strong relationship with it.

Of Wideman's recent books, *Brothers* provides a nonfictional medium that allows Wideman to strengthen the relationship and to declare his own allegiance, and that of the black intellectual, unmistakably to the community. This allegiance frees Wideman and the intellectual from anxiety regarding their lofty flights and formal experimentation; their allegiance to the community dictates that they must seek to help it however they can. In *Reuben*, the intellectual assists the community by shaping and voicing postmodernism in a way that can aid black people in their daily struggles against hardship and oppression.

John Edgar Wideman was born on June 14, 1941, in Washington, D.C. but spent his formative years in the Homewood section of Pittsburgh. He was the son of a waiter in a poor but largely stable black neighborhood; his parents were economically marginal but self-supporting. Wideman has said little about his formative years through junior high school. He apparently started to develop intellectually and to isolate himself in a white world away from the black community during high school. At this time his parents managed to move the family from Homewood into Shadyside, a more well-to-do neighborhood. There Wideman attended the racially integrated Peabody High School, starred on the basketball team, became president of the senior class, and was named valedictorian. At Peabody, Wideman began to develop the habits that would bring him early success as a writer but would also be the source of inner torment.

Wideman at first identified strongly with white academe and tried to prevent his black experience from intruding. He evidently found the two worlds incompatible and tried to keep them separate while he concentrated on his academic progress. He started to compartmentalize his psyche, creating a black section and a white section, and followed suit in his actions. Racial tension was apparently in the air at Peabody, and according to one account given years later by a classmate, Wideman reacted with a subterfuge that somewhat recalls Richard Wright's *Black Boy*, which is set in the American South several decades earlier. Wideman was unwilling to be seen on the street alone with a white girl and would not walk to classes with white students. He spent his time out of class with other black students, and then moved into the white academic world when class began (Plummer 1985:124). In this way Wideman split himself in two. His inner compartmentalization became a source of anguish, as it isolated him from the black community.

At the University of Pennsylvania, where Wideman received a full athletic scholarship and majored in English, he further developed his technique for dividing himself into parts. He learned to become invisible and played the game that Ralph Ellison's Invisible Man learned in *Invisible Man*, although Wideman had not read Ellison's book at the time. Wideman always kept a black friend on the side, but he spent a distinct part of his life with white athletic friends, who, like him, were members of the University of Pennsylvania basketball team, and with white academic friends. Wideman has said, "Living that kind of life . . . was a performance. It was like buying tickets of admission and paying with little pieces of yourself" (Plummer 1985:124, 127). When his undergraduate years at the University of Pennsylvania ended in 1963, Wideman won a Rhodes

Scholarship. His time at Oxford University did nothing to change the pattern that I have described.

Wideman was one of the first two black Rhodes scholars in more than fifty years to carry out the term at Oxford. Afterward he returned to the University of Pennsylvania to become the first tenured black professor in the school's history. He started to read black literature during this time and began at least tentatively to reorient himself as a black man and writer, but he continued to struggle with the reality of his isolation from black people. His wife, Judy, says, "In the '60's . . . there was a gradual willingness on John's part to look at himself and his background. It was painful, difficult for him to do. In order to achieve the things he'd done, he'd had to look away. The difference between where he was and where his family was was very difficult for him to reconcile" (Plummer 1985:127).

Wideman left Pennsylvania with his wife, Judy, whom he married in 1965, and his two sons and took a job in the English Department at the University of Wyoming in Laramie, Wyoming. There his children could grow up safe from the hazards of the Philadelphia streets. The move in many ways exacerbated Wideman's problem because it increased the physical distance from his family and the black community. He did not start to break down his psychological walls and to bridge the long, open space between Laramie and Homewood until after his grandmother's funeral in Homewood in 1973. Then he began to listen closely to the stories his relatives told, positive, supportive tales of family and the Homewood community (Plummer 1985:127–28). The stories, imbued as they were with black tradition, helped revitalize his fiction and at the same time reoriented him in relation to black experience. Partly as a result of these stories, then, Wideman began to reintegrate himself into the black community. As his recent statements about his position in the 1980s indicate, Wideman is the writer-intellectual who has overcome his alienation and returned home.

In *Brothers*, the character John, who is the younger Wideman, describes how, as a writer, he has isolated himself from the black community. According to John, in his imagination he has created a fictional sanctuary using white, Western ideas, literature, and art; outside this sanctuary lies the rich, elusive reality of the black community as seen by various black people and as projected through their lives. John embodies within himself a series of dichotomies: imagination versus reality, inside versus outside, and individual black intellectual versus the black community. That is, John's imaginative inner black intellectual self often creates brilliantly but is disengaged from the problematic, rich, evasive reality of the black community, with which John is very uncomfortable. In section 2 of *Brothers*, John asks himself an important question: "Do I write to escape, to make fiction of my life?" The text of *Brothers* clearly answers yes, John must stop trying to escape his blackness and must stop making this kind of "fiction of my life." In *Brothers*, the experience of John's brother Robby, who, unlike John, stayed in the community but was unfortunate enough to be imprisoned for life without the possibility of parole, encompasses many aspects of the contemporary black community as it must appear to a young black man. John avoids Robby by isolating himself in the literary world of the writer-intellectual, a withdrawal that is tantamount to an escape from the black community.

At the end of the book, a bond develops between the brothers. John starts to see the world in many of the same ways that Robby does—and in ways with which many blacks would agree or sympathize. Implicit in the bond that develops between the two brothers is the idea that they share in and feel allegiance to the same black community, which has much good and much potential despite the troubled times that have overtaken it. John selfishly left his brother and the community, disregarding his responsibility to them. In *Brothers* we see John return, ready to discharge his responsibilities. In the course of his professional development as a writer, Wideman has uncovered valuable resources for overcoming the barriers to activism that exist within the black intellectual and within the black community.

A Glance Away

White Writers and the Modernist Influence

In *A Glance Away*, the first of the early books, Wideman uses mainstream modernist literary tradition to develop his craft (O'Brien 1973:215). His articulation of a modernism that derives from T. S. Eliot and other white literary masters dominates the book. In *Glance*, Wideman presents the same black family (his own) (Samuels 1983:42) and black community (Homewood) of which we are to hear in the Homewood trilogy and in *Brothers and Keepers*, but Robert Thurley, a white intellectual alienated from the black and white communities, is the main character and a figure who clearly recalls Eliot's Prufrock and Gerontion. More than anything, a general pattern of twentieth-century cultural and societal ennui, ineffectuality, fear, and failure affects Thurley. Thurley's dominance in *Glance* and the association of the quality of the blacks' lives with Thurley's places *Glance* in the mainstream modernist literary tradition and precludes a broader treatment of black life. Wideman, in other words, fails to achieve a black voicing of modernism, as he was to do in the Homewood trilogy and *Brothers and Keepers,* because he does not create an authentic black diction, cadence, and rhythm for his characters' speech and does not draw on black cultural tradition as a source of relief from oppression, suffering, and pessimism in racist America. Wideman's concern with a white intellectual character in the modernist tradition of T. S. Eliot's effete intellectuals also prevents him from focusing on the theme of the black intellectual's alienation from the black community. *Glance* shows Wideman deeply immersed in white modernism.

Wideman's construction of language at the beginning of *Glance*'s Prologue indicates that he gives secondary priority to recreating black speech. The first several paragraphs of the prologue read as follows:

> It is afterall a way of beginning. To have never quite enough so hunger grows faster than appetites and satisfaction never comes.
>
> On an April day insouciant after the fashion of spring insouciance the warm secret of life was shared with another. Bawling milk hungry mammal dropped in pain from flanks of a she. Him.
>
> Fine, healthy boy, eight pound seven ounces.
>
> Mystery repeats itself to boredom. And he shall be called Eugene. In the name of the grandfather who balding, high on dago red, waited news in a cloud of garbage smelling smoke at the foot of steep, ringing marble stairs of Allegheny General Hospital.
>
> —Wonder what they's doing to my littlebaby. Martha better be all right. Freeda, I got me a grandson. Big 'un he's gonna be. Big and bad like his granddaddy Eugene. A big, bad niggerGene, said the tall bald pate man clomping on bunioned feet loudly up the stairs, shrugging off tentative back holding hands and small voice excited of pale receptionist starched white at desk. A bigniggerGene.
>
> —You can't go up there sir.
>
> —My little girl's up there lady. You hear me, my little Martha's there and nobody on God's green earth's gonna keep me from my girl. Off shuffling to tune of *Gimme* that *wine spudie-udie* he went, dedecorumed in glee of life bearing his name, his flesh and blood redone forever in two bodies precious together under hospital blankets. [3][1]

The passage's most important aspect is Wideman's manipulation of his materials to create a modernist form that does not include genuine black speech. The form here is not as radical as in the stream-of-consciousness section at the end of *Glance* or in parts of Wideman's other books. But Wideman is still obviously trying to use language in unconventional ways so that the reader will view a possibly familiar scene differently. Wideman inverts the order of words ("shrugging off tentative back holding hands and small voice excited") and shapes single words for special effects ("bigniggerGene" and "dedecorumed").

Part of the language and experience here is black, but the black aspect is secondary to Wideman's creation of a mainstream modernist reality. The word "nigger" is obviously associated with the black experience, but not much else is so obviously black. As far as other choices of language and rhythm of language are concerned, "Big 'un he's gonna be," in the fifth paragraph, for example, does not sound accurate and suggestive of black speech; and "Wonder what they's doing to my littlebaby," and the other words of DaddyGene in this passage, are not distinctively black enough to capture a sense of genuine black speech.

Wideman's articulation of a dominant mainstream modernist vision of the world that, among twentieth-century white literary masters, is most reminiscent of poet T. S. Eliot mainly precludes a black voicing of modernism in the book, however. Thurley echoes "Gerontion" and speaks of Eliot as he ruminates about action and resignation.

> Once past it [innocence], the wish can only be in terms of choosing life or death, to stop or go on. The poem [that one creates] becomes an oasis, a sort of gas station that is only sought because it provides the means of going on, not a destination. . . . *an old man in a dry month, being read to by a boy,* for some reason as they often did, the lives came to Thurley. They broke into the mild self-satisfaction he felt with his gas station metaphor. Eliot was for him the poet of wariness, of old age. His frightened old men had aged the undergraduate Thurley prematurely and strangely, they now came back bringing Thurley a poignant youth. It had all gone so quickly. Between two readings of a poem his lifetime had nearly slipped away. Sometimes it seemed like that. That only a few events, insignificant on any objective scale but emotionally changed beyond calculation had been crowded into a morning and afternoon, a poignantly recent time, so close it seemed that now as he sat in a long evening of recollection something still could be done. But he knew once gone was always gone, time past had no minutes or years. In fact, it seemed colors were much more adequate to describe his fast receding day, blues, reds, yellows, violets, a glowing spectrum from blazing white to the black of night. [154]

Thurley's problem, of course, is that his life is a waste. He is an alcoholic homosexual professor whose great learning serves him very little. He is totally ineffective in the classroom and depends on homosexual affairs with poor blacks whom he picks up in bars. His ineffectuality is evident from the scene involving a love-making triangle consisting of Thurley, his wife, and Thurley's best friend, Al. Thurley felt humiliated, watching his friend make love to his wife. But the wife had made Thurley feel totally inadequate, and he felt he could do nothing but yield to her demand for a love triangle. With his sexual ineptitude and failure, Thurley recalls not only Gerontion and Prufrock but various people throughout *The Waste Land*, too.

Most important, Thurley projects much of the book's vision, theme, and possible resolution. At the end, Thurley breaks out of his Prufrockian shell of ineffectuality and tries to inspire Eddie, who has just returned from drug treatment, and who is in deep despair because he believes he has caused his mother's death. Central in the book is Thurley's transformation from a weak, lost, constantly humiliated white intellectual and professor to a man of courage and responsibility who reaches out to save a poor black man. Much of the vision is early Eliot.

White modernist vision also subsumes the other characters in *Glance. Glance*'s characters are stuck in the past and are unable to face life in the present. They are frightened by old age and paralyzed by alienation, frustration, and anger. Eddie's mother Martha is an angry, frustrated, physically paralyzed old woman who has not felt really alive since the death during the war of her oldest son, Eugene. She is highly dissatisfied with her daughter, Bette, and son Eddie and seems to hate everything else around her, including Eddie's best friend, Brother, and a harmless family dog. Most of the book takes place on an Easter Sunday when Eddie returns from drug treatment. It is implied that Eddie, Martha, and the others may be resurrected. But Martha, her lower body locked in steel braces and her mind locked in evil and pessimistic thought, remains spiritually dead.

> Something roared in the old woman's ears. It rose a crescendo of surging, deep throated sound. Like sea shells clamped to both ears the room possessed her in its blank ubiquitous rhythm. From some unknown source, far out of her own experience and reaching back to a dark communal fund of impulse she sensed the warning of this ocean sound. The deadness below her waist climbed inch by inch to turn her whole body into stone. It was only Bette's hands on her shoulders and the violent rocking of her body back and forth in her son's grasp that woke her to the sound of her own low keening—nothing . . . nothing . . . nothing . . . nothing. [98]

Martha cannot respond to Eddie during this cold, spiritless Easter supper at home. She concludes Easter Sunday by falling down the stairs, physically dead.

Eddie's sister, Bette, is a victim of their mother's frustration and anger. She spends her life taking care of Martha and perpetually encounters Martha's resentment and her charges that she is Brother Tate's whore. Just before Martha dies, Eddie tries to persuade Bette to entrust Martha to a nurse and to go away where she, Bette, can learn to enjoy her life. Bette is fearful and unable to imagine leaving their mother without anyone to take care of her. Her attitude is clearly humane, but it is also clear that she does not understand her own need and that of her brother to live vitally. Bette's life has been a waste and is essentially over.

The character Brother Tate also appears in *Sent for You Yesterday.* Although he is physically similar in the two books, he is substantially different. Whereas in *Yesterday* Brother embodies much of the strength and depth of the black community, in *Glance* he merely dabbles in dope and homosexual sex and is someone who lacks a clear direction. He is truly Eddie's friend and is reasonably kind to Thurley, but what he offers either one of them is limited. For Thurley, he is a pickup when Thurley is slumming and wallowing in degradation in black bars, and he is a connection to Eddie. He is there when Eddie needs him, but after Eddie's mother's death, when Eddie blames himself, Brother can only advise him to return to dope, the only source of solace that Brother recognizes. Although innocuous and well meaning, Brother is as lost and directionless as the other black characters in the book.

Sickness, death, and alienation have dominated Eddie's recent life. Eddie's slide into drug abuse, jail, and drug rehabilitation began after the death of his father and brother Eugene during a time when his mother only wanted Eugene, the eldest son whom she preferred. Living in a void where he could not be the object of his mother's love, Eddie felt neglected and sought sustenance elsewhere. This sustenance was first alcohol and then drugs.

Wideman is aware that constructive black traditions and rituals exist that could, perhaps, allow his black characters to transcend their alienation, fear, frustration, and anger, but he allows the mainstream white modernist dead-end pessimism to remain dominant. Wideman suggests that supportive black family and community traditions cannot function for Eddie in the face of pessimism and failure. Eddie tries to place himself, his younger sister Bette, and community traditions in the context of a story of the black community-oriented Sanctified Church services to which Grandfather DaddyGene introduced him. But Eddie cannot successfully finish the story because he cannot hold the sustaining vision (127–28). Eddie's loss of the vision severs any link that connects him and Bette with potentially sustaining community traditions. In the Homewood trilogy, stories like the one that Eddie tries to tell Bette become the source of true sustenance that maintains and strengthens people in the face of hardship and adversity and form an important part of the black voicing of a black worldview. Here black stories and storytelling rituals afford no sustenance, and the articulation of mainstream modernist reality silences a black voicing of a supportive black cultural form and ritual.

In his determination to develop as a writer by exploring the mainstream modernist tradition, Wideman stresses pessimism and ineffectuality in his depiction of Eddie's family. Eddie is in a hopeless situation, so immersed in a cold, spiritless reality that he cannot possibly extricate himself. It is selfish and inhumane for him and Bette to leave Martha, as Eddie advises, but they both face sure spiritual death if they do not leave. Martha's physical death eliminates the possibilities of family revival unless Eddie and Bette can show an ability to take action that will allow them to live vital lives on their own. Black cultural traditions and their influence are conspicuously absent.

As previously noted, Wideman's language structure, created to depict an unfamiliar reality, is less radical than it becomes in later books, although Wideman does give it priority over the rendering of black language, which he keeps in the background. In *Glance*, Wideman adheres closely to a mainstream literary pattern which prevents modernist concerns from being voiced by blacks. The overall presentation of the story through *Glance*'s three-part structure demonstrates Wideman's adherence to mainstream modernism.

Wideman demonstrates his commitment to white tradition in the first section. The first twelve pages of section 1 sustain the focus on Eddie's family that was evident in the prologue, detailing the early part of his return from dope rehabilitation. Then the narrative switches to a portrayal of Robert Thurley. Here Wideman's intention of developing a mainstream modernist focus begins to emerge. He has begun with black life in the prologue and early part of section 1, but he now starts to make black life subordinate. At this point in Wideman's career, the tension between white intellectual tradition and black tradition is resolved in favor of white tradition.

After Thurley's introduction early in section 1, his life becomes central and his vision sets the tone for the rest of the book. The problems of the black family assume the quality of Thurley's problems and the color of his vision. The sordidness and wastefulness of Thurley's life attach to Eddie through his relationship with Thurley, and waste, frustration, and ineffectuality pervade Eddie's family in the present, as opposed to the past, when DaddyGene, his wife, Freeda, and Clarence were alive and life was happier. The bleakness and pessimism of the family situation are apparent in section 1 as Eddie meets his mother upon his return, and we see her bitter, cold reactions to everyone and Bette's blighted spirit under her vitriolic influence.

Section 2 carries on the pessimistic modernist theme. Most of section 2 deals with Eddie's family and the comparison between the happy past and the bitter, frustrated present. The culminating event for the family in this section is Martha's death.

At the end of section 2, the narrative shifts in a way that recalls the ending of Eliot's *The Waste Land.* After an Easter chapel service which has inspired him, Thurley feels the promise of renewal and rebirth.

> Thurley wanted to feel the wind, wanted it to lap inside his clothes and finger his body. The blossoms swam by his eyes. Jerky, uneven movements as they circled closer to the earth. Shuddering it seemed as a puff of air shot them forward, then suddenly dropped its support. It would rain soon, and the puddles would be thick with white blossoms. They would float, mixing with the scum and acrid green to form mottled rainbows in stagnant pools. The air brought its message of rain in a cool draft across Thurley's perspiring face. As he walked, clouds clustered around the sun, and long tree shadows disappeared insensibly into the general darkness. [145]

"The air brought its message in a cool draft across Thurley's perspiring face. . . . clouds clustered around the sun" clearly parallels lines carrying the promise of renewal near the end of *The Waste Land:* "Then a damp gust / Bringing rain / . . . / while the black clouds / Gathered far distant" (Eliot 1934:44–45). Also, Thurley's potential renewal and rebirth after his apparently hopeless spiritual stagnation throughout the first two sections are ironic, just as the potential for renewal and rebirth at the end of *The Waste Land* is ironic after the poem's seemingly hopeless blight and pessimism.

In section 3, furthermore, no black voice articulates black tradition and its role. As before, black experience continues to move in the direction of mainstream modernist, white literary vision. Thurley becomes a possible means to Eddie's resurrection, someone who can inspire him with the courage and strength to face life. Just as mainstream modernism obscures black tradition at the beginning of *Glance*, Eddie's life at the end follows the tortured, agonized hope held out by Thurley, a figure modeled after literary figures in white modernist literary texts.

The portrayal of black life is pale; Wideman makes mainstream modernist themes so dominant that they preclude any possible black traditional views about and responses to problems. Wideman later laments this dominance (Samuels 1983:43–44, 58–59) and tries to create books that will explore black life deeply and will influence black people. But this treatment of mainstream modernism and black tradition is characteristic of his early career.

In at least one episode in *Glance*, however, Wideman brings uniquely black responses and attitudes into the foreground. When Eddie returns from drug rehabilitation on Easter Sunday, he tries to rekindle his relationship with Brother's sister Alice, but Alice cannot forgive him for his affair with a white girl, Clara, during the time when she and Eddie were going together.

> —You can't forget can you. One night, Alice, one lousy night. Clara getting her kicks and me like a fool obliging. I didn't think you'd ever know, and even if you did, I didn't see how you could care. She's a tramp, you know that. She just wanted a toss in the hay.
> —With her black buck. With you so she could smile and proclaim it. So she could prove her principles with what she has between her legs. No, no I didn't care, it didn't matter to me sitting listening every time she opened her mouth to how real it was, to how meaningful it was, to all the essential truths it demonstrated about men and women. Her glib, bitch mouth so full of praise for Edward, how tender he was, how understanding, how it didn't make any difference in the world what color he was. No . . . It didn't matter; I didn't care.
> —Once, Alice, once, I swear it. That's all. I never touched her again.
> —Do you think it matters—how many times mattered. I gave you something, I trusted you Eddie. And all I gave you were willing to trade with that whore for a smell of her white ass. She cried, bitterly and for an age it seemed. [118–19]

Alice probably feels that it would have been bad for Eddie to be unfaithful with any woman, but the fact that he had an affair with a white woman greatly exacerbates the problem. Many black women feel a special and deep loathing for black men and white women

who engage in intercourse, especially when the black women think
that they have been exploited in the process.

Such feelings originate in the black woman's long-standing belief
that she is doubly victimized by the black man who responds to his
oppression at the hands of the white man by having sexual relations
with the white woman. In the "Black Macho" section of *Black
Macho and the Myth of the Superwoman* (1980), Michelle Wallace
discusses the black woman's outrage with the black man because of
his inability to counter the white man's attempt to emasculate him.
In his attempt to respond to the white man's oppression, the black
man tries to prove his manhood sexually with the white woman and
at the same time tries to demonstrate equality with the white man
by making his own woman, the black woman, submit to his will
during the whole process. The black woman's greatest outrage is the
black man's conspiracy with the white woman that makes the black
woman a victim once again. Although Alice may not be consciously
reasoning in this way, Wallace portrays many of the attitudes and
feelings of black women such as Alice.

Wideman presents black responses in this episode, but they do not
significantly change the mainstream modernist thematic structure
of *Glance.* Alice's feelings and responses clearly stay within
Glance's catalogue of unameliorated frustrations, pain, and anger.
Wideman offers no range of black rituals, beliefs, and traditions that
would help Alice and the other characters cope with their situation
and sustain them in their hardship. The articulation of such rituals,
beliefs, and traditions in the context of hardship and suffering would
constitute a black voicing of modernist concerns.

Throughout this chapter I have emphasized Wideman's failure to develop the black voice that is the key to his mature writing
in the Homewood trilogy and the recent books. One reason is that
Wideman had not read other black writers who had achieved a black
voicing of common mainstream modernist and black themes. In the
mid-1960s, when Wideman was writing *Glance,* he had at best a
passing acquaintance with the work of Richard Wright and Ralph
Ellison (Samuels 1983:44). At this time, several of the contemporary
black writers on whom Wideman would later draw had published
little, if anything. Still, Wideman had available to him the work of
an older writer—Ellison—and that of a contemporary, William
Melvin Kelley. Close attention to Ellison and Kelley would have
shown Wideman what he did not discover until later, during his
prolonged period of reading, that a writer can combine mainstream

modernism and black tradition and achieve a black voicing of modernism. Certainly this statement is true of Ellison's *Invisible Man* (1952). Ellison combines modernist, existentialist chaos and corruption with black cultural tradition to show how the tradition can ameliorate the bad effects of racial oppression and life in the generally oppressive modern world. Kelley might have been an even better example for Wideman because, like Wideman, he completely occupied himself with the study of white Western tradition early in his life and did not become aware of black social issues until he was in his late twenties (Barksdale and Kinnamon 1972:795). Kelley's second and third novels, *Dancers on the Shore* (1964) and *A Drop of Patience* (1965), which may have been available to Wideman when he wrote *Glance*, show a progressive development into the exploration of black racial issues and black culture. From the beginning, Kelley experimented with mainstream modernist fictional forms, and he successfully combined these forms with an increasing emphasis on black life as his career developed.

Thus far I have stressed *Glance*'s shortcomings by comparison with Wideman's mature work in the Homewood trilogy and the recent books. *Glance* is nevertheless impressive as a first novel in which the writer is developing his craft. Some of *Glance*'s formal qualities are noteworthy. These same mainstream modernist formal qualities, when combined with a black voice speaking from the richness of black culture, will later serve Wideman well in present-ing substantive, in-depth portrayals of black life.

In *Glance* Wideman skillfully uses the stream-of-consciousness technique, by which he explores what Robert Humphrey calls the characters' "prespeech levels of consciousness" to reveal their "psy-chic being" (Humphrey 1954:4). The psyches of his characters are more important in *Hurry Home* and *The Lynchers*, but Wideman also captures the minds and thoughts of his characters in *Glance*.

Wideman draws on different writers in creating his stream-of-consciousness technique. He sometimes borrows from and echoes William Faulkner and James Joyce, for example. Specifically, in *Glance*, the technique at times parallels that in Faulkner, and some of Brother's characteristic thinking may recall Benjy's in *The Sound and the Fury* (Frazier 1975:26–27). But the way in which the characters' thinking in the present triggers and merges with thoughts from the past, and the way in which thinking and com-ment in the present display general relevance for and association with events over time, reflect stream-of-consciousness techniques that Wideman shares with several writers (Frazier 1975:24–26). Wideman is drawing on modernist technique and shaping it to fit the contours of his own fiction.

Wideman experiments by using the stream-of-consciousness technique in unusual ways when, at the end of *Glance*, characters' thought replaces dialogue and links characters. At the end of *Glance*, Thurley, Eddie, and Brother sit around a fire in the hobo's forest.

> But I must be heard, must be seen. I must say I am not afraid. These rocks, I cannot let him leave the fire.
>
> Bette screams. She cannot lift [Martha after she falls down the steps]. She tries but cannot lift. Two heavy, too heavy for Bette to lift. For me . . .
>
> If he starts to get up, if he moves away from the fire into the darkness again I will grab. . . . I will make him carry me through the night. If only I could say something. . . . if words were only made to touch. . . . if only for a moment. I had the singer's voice [who sang at the chapel earlier that Easter Sunday], the beauty of her voice I believe I could make him understand.
>
> A little girl . . . I must . . . lift . . . help her lift.
>
> It will come, it will follow, morning will. . . . and the strength . . . witness . . . I have been through, climbed through the night, the darkness . . . I have been there and now. . . , now I see.
>
> Bette tries, like a little girl's falling, she tries, she raises Mama in her arms.
>
> Floating, a gull over the blue lake.
>
> Bette whispers, I think she is whispering, but it is because she has no breath because she cannot say the word, because it is her mother who lies there.
>
> The strength . . . the light radiant on his back . . . morning.
>
> Bette screams. All time. The stone's hard push into my back, the fire crackling. Daddy's coming. . . . soon he'll be here. No more time, no more waiting soon soon it pushes, it is hard to sit alone, to feed it, to watch it die, something . . . nothing . . . flame. [185–86]

Throughout this quotation the stream-of-consciousness technique traces the thoughts in the minds of Eddie and Thurley. Thurley first thinks about his need to speak and to inspire Eddie with his newfound courage. Then, in the following paragraph, Eddie thinks about his mother's death. The paragraphs alternate as Thurley continues to agonize with the desire to sustain Eddie through the night and Eddie totally occupies himself with his mother's death and with Bette's reaction to it.

In the last paragraph of the quoted passage, Wideman pushes the technique further than most writers except perhaps Faulkner in *The Sound and the Fury*. The first three phrases and clauses in this paragraph ("Bette screams. All time. The stone's hard push into my back") focus on Eddie's thinking as he grieves for his mother, Bette, and his family and also on Thurley's thinking as he tries to make his wish to fortify Eddie tangible, like the stone's hardness in his back and the crackle of the fire. The thinking of Eddie and Thurley merges here, and the merging of thoughts serves as attachment, as communication between the characters. Through his thoughts, Thurley gives Eddie sustenance as the flame symbolically flickers, dies, and glows ("something . . . nothing . . . flame").

The thoughts of the characters continue.

> If Eddie moves I will cling; he will have to drag me. Hold on even to the edge . . .
> They don't move. They cannot speak. The flame crackles. I don't move, don't speak. All time, near then far, near then far, near then far. The crickets stop. We are part of the fire. We are part of the silence. I cannot move. I cannot speak. [186]

The second paragraph in this quotation shows the way in which the thought of the characters merges and the way in which Thurley communicates strength to Eddie through thought. The speaker believes that they are both now "part of the fire," and although at the end the speaker, probably Thurley, "cannot move. . . , cannot speak," there is still strength in their mental communication and attachment.

Brother strengthens the bond further when he brings the three of them together in his reverie at the end of the book.

> *I wonder how far it [the sky] is somebody should find out and tell people cause I'm sure they want to know look at them both closer to my fire now and both looking at the flames I wonder what it feels like to burn if it always hurts once your hand is in it deep if it pops and sparks like wood and if the color is the same and if it hurts where does it go if you keep it in smoke rises through the trees to the sky towards the black roof where the sun will come if the sun comes tomorrow does it hurt or smell and how high up the smoke kids do it stick their hands right in you gotta keep them away or they'll do it like bugs who get too close and burn up I see why they try once why they want to touch I can see it in Eddie's eyes in the white man's eyes that stare at the flame they want to touch to put them in and see if it keeps hurting I can understand why kids do it cause I want to touch myself just like one I want to put my hand in I want to go to smoke and see how high. [186]*

In the passage quoted, Wideman suggests the unfamiliar-looking and unfamiliar-sounding regions of the characters' minds mainly through elliptical language constructions and free-flowing, un-punctuated sentences. Particularly noteworthy, however, is the way in which Wideman adds a twist to the form by making the thought serve functionally as a medium for communication in the para-graphs where the characters' thoughts merge. In the overall context of a book that often uses a mainstream modernist form to depict an abstract, unfamiliar reality, the stream-of-consciousness technique serves Wideman well.

Although he had not yet developed a black voice, the twenty-six-year-old Wideman had achieved a great deal by the time he wrote *Glance.* His preoccupation with modernism had good effects as well as bad. His modernist form is occasionally impressive; the tech-niques exhibited here would later contribute to Wideman's black voicing of modernism. With the publication of *Glance,* Wideman showed that a budding talent was at work.

1. Unless otherwise noted, works quoted are by Wideman. Parenthetical or bracketed numbers refer to pages in the editions listed in the References.

Hurry Home

The Black Intellectual Uncertain and Confused

Hurry Home, the second of Wideman's early books, takes as its point of departure Wideman's uncertainty and ambivalence about the black writer-intellectual's alienation from the black community. *Home* marks a progression from the author's position in *Glance* because in it for the first time Wideman treats the black intellectual's alienation and makes a black the central character. In addition, however, *Home* shows Wideman the writer-intellectual caught in mainstream modernism; the black intellectual's alienation is still largely expressed in the mainstream modernist voice. *Home* uses mainstream modernist forms to articulate the main character's fantasy world of fear, failure, horror, uncertainty, and ambivalence, which he partly creates, ironically, to insulate himself from the black community in his isolated sanctuary. *Home* seldom articulates black rituals, cultural forms, and traditions that would help Cecil cope with his problems and perhaps provide a bridge to the community. Wideman fails to combine mainstream modernism and black tradition in a way that would produce a black voice in *Home*, as he fails to do in *Glance*. It should not be forgotten, however, that *Home* makes a black intellectual central rather than a white one, and this is Wideman's first step toward making black life, and later black cultural tradition, the center of his work. Wideman's portrayal of the alienated black intellectual is often gripping and thought provoking. Also, Wideman further develops his skill with mainstream modernist forms that he will later combine with black forms and traditions.

Paradoxes that stem from the main character's uncertainty and confusion and the uncertainty, ambivalence, and irony in the narrative viewpoint, and also become more evident and powerful as the book progresses, lay the thematic foundation for *Home*. One paradox is that the narrative viewpoint both condemns the main character and other characters who live in confused fantasy worlds and pardons them because they seem to be doing the best they can under the circumstances. Another paradox is that the main character, as a black intellectual, feels the need to isolate himself from the black community and pursue his intellectual life. But at the same time, isolation produces in the main character lingering memories of the black tradition and even more pain, suffering, and agony than he experienced while in contact with the black community, evidence of the need for him to come out of isolation and live with other blacks.

The main character, Cecil Braithwaite, much like Wideman himself, embodies the dichotomy between the individual black intellectual and the black community. He uses his imagination to create a sanctuary sheltered from the immediate reality of his black community. This sanctuary is a fluid, open-ended world where Cecil can indulge in modernist fantasies; he tinkers with the possibility of altering and shaping the reality of himself and sometimes seems to derive a masochistic pleasure from subjecting himself to nightmarish fantasies and experiences. Cecil's fantasies are modernist and not postmodernist; Cecil would actually like to change external reality through his fantasies. He is looking for more than subjective fulfillment. Cecil believes his own words or at least tries to believe his own words. He is not consciously creating fictions.

Cecil uses the tragedy of his infant son's death to center his imagination and tutors it with a law school education, historical knowledge, white literature, and European art, primarily the Hieronymus Bosch painting *The Garden of Delights*. The book's epigraph, from Stephane Mallarmé, in part reads *ce mal d'être deux* ("the pain of being two") (Marcus 1986:322). Cecil is indeed of two minds but tries to focus his imagination on whiteness and to separate it from blackness.

While the black community in *Glance* was superficial and took second place to mainstream modernist intellectual ideas, Cecil finds the black community burdensome and oppressive. He feels that he must escape it. He isolates himself from the community, subjects himself to its ostracism, and makes himself pretentious and ridiculous in the process. Cecil does not believe that an educated black man like himself can find fulfillment and comfort in the community; black people will only drag him down. Cecil draws upon his white, Western training, and whatever else he needs, to create the modernist fantasies that will occupy his mind and will thus allow him to escape the immediate reality of the black community.

Home's viewpoint questions this perspective and gains strength as *Home* progresses. A sensitive indicator of irony and ambivalence, this viewpoint establishes a paradox and helps to complicate *Home*. Very early in *Home*, Cecil imaginatively tries to escape any fixity that will define him and then to escape the oppressive reality of blackness outside himself. The first five pages of the book set forth many references to dream, intangibility, and lack of reality. Then Cecil calls himself many different ghosts (6). Later in the first section, it becomes clear that Cecil would, if he could, use words to transform himself so that he would not be black.

> Mirror said time was Cecil when you could not see your face unless someone lifted you to broken glass above the sink. . . . then one day saw wooly hair and dust that wouldn't wash off you saw colored boy Cecil and really surprised you saw something you had no way of knowing different or worse you saw your face and knew the dust would not change and now you see all things go away but that doesn't go away wooly hair creeps back on your forehead, but only reveals more dust beneath you will always be dying Cecil but that will not die. . . . He wondered why he hadn't thought of libraries before [he has deserted his wife and, temporarily, taken refuge in a library for a day]. Perhaps they were rooted too deeply in the other element—books and silent cubicles, alcoves stale with page dust and nervous, muffled breath as word kindled in dry heatless extinction. Word become flesh become Cecil become invisible opener of doors, lightener of burden, of care, of pigmentation even, transforming

mirror Cecil to that which only if you try hard can you find between black parenthesis of mortar board and gown. [17–18]

Cecil makes himself ridiculous here by wanting to change his blackness; it is of course a physical impossibility to do so. The "dust that wouldn't wash off" is Cecil's blackness, and this blackness is inerasable and oppressive. But if the word could transform, could "become flesh become Cecil"—if Cecil could lose himself in an imaginative fantasy created through words—then he could escape the "burden" of his blackness. He can create a kind of secure place by manipulating words that degrees alone ("black parenthesis of mortar board and gown") cannot create. The quoted passage echoes Eliot's "Gerontion," in which Gerontion talks about multiplying "variety / In a Wilderness of mirrors" (Eliot 1934:21). And the latter part of the quotation also draws on lines in the poem preceding those just quoted: "Signs are taken for wonders. 'We would see a sign!' / The word within a word, unable to speak a word, / Swaddled with darkness" (1934:19). The reference to Eliot supports the point about Cecil being ridiculous. Very generally, he appears ridiculous, as Gerontion does.

Immediately after the passage quoted above, Wideman presents a series of images and descriptions that further demonstrates Cecil's aversion to blackness. The first image develops out of Cecil's memory of a drawing of St. Barbara in a green dress, her dress spreading, "a lush growing thing on the hillside, [as] she gazes up from a book, quill in hand." The next image grows out of Cecil's memory of a black woman in a lighted window, "naked, not giving a fuck, guzzling whisky from a bottle. Life's done this to me she said and life is your eyes taking me in" (18–19). The contrast in the images, the white one rich, contemplative, productive, the black one bawdy, uncouth, unattractive, is clear. On the same street where Cecil saw the black woman, he sees a black family at a railroad station awaiting the arrival of the casket of another family member. Cecil's tone is mocking as he watches the family of blacks and thinks that soon they will begin to sing, evidently to Cecil a futile exercise in the face of death and their black reality. Later in the first section, Cecil again mocks black humility, faith, and perseverance in the image of old Elder Watkins, a faithful one in the black church who has sat at the feet of Reverend Reed, intoning scriptures to make the gates of heaven open. Cecil remembers Elder Watkins's age and poverty and thinks he could be a "tattered shade of a black Polonius, of ignorance [he cannot read or write] and desperate dignity done to death like a rat" (26). Cecil contrasts Reverend Reed, Elder Watkins, and Easter service at the black church with Easter service at the white Presbyterian church, where they are singing a song by a "German you [Reverend Reed and Elder Watkins] should have known. Heinrich Schütz, who would surely recognize that Jesus shuffle of yours beneath a cross of dignity" (26). Cecil did not disturb Elder Watkins on the day he remembers seeing him but went on to the Presbyterian church to hear the St. John Passion of Schütz.

In this section, Cecil is reacting to black people with the high-brow attitude of the superior educated man. He has educated himself to the point where he can understand and appreciate the Van Eyckian drawing of St. Barbara and the music of Schütz; this appreciation for high culture makes him reject black vulgarity and mock grass-roots black religious belief and practice.

In overall tone the narrative starts to assume an ambivalence and uncertainty but is not totally critical of Cecil. In the passage where Cecil studies his mirror image, the narrative carries a cutting, ironic tone: "Then one day [you] saw colored boy Cecil and really surprised you saw something you had no way of knowing different or worse you saw your face and knew the dust would not change and now you see all things go away but that doesn't go away." Cecil is serious about his problems with his blackness, but the narrative mocks him for being shocked at seeing the "colored boy" and surprised at seeing the blackness that will not come off.

The narrative tone in the passage where Cecil looks through the window at the naked black woman, however, is more sympathetic to his plight.

> Cecil knew he would see her again. As he approached a rare lighted window each time he thought she would be there again. Something moved her in endless visitations through the rooms of the narrow row houses just as it moved him along the Black pavement that was a ribbon around them. She was the fat, pink owner and the exploited tenant just as Cecil was the echo and sound of his night wanderings. No one had wed them, no one had even introduced them and yet they were blind lovers eternally bound. Cecil and the lady, Cecil sound and Cecil echo, landlord and tenant. [19]

Cecil, the wanderer, the runner from blackness, runs a course parallel to that of the exploited black woman. They are both victims, both out of control of their destiny. Cecil may be blind and misguided, but the narrative here does not criticize or mock him.

The narrative starts to take on the tone of uncertainty and ambivalence that, together with Cecil's uncertainty and ambivalence, will later highlight the book's central paradoxes. One passage criticizes Cecil for wanting to evade his blackness; the other suggests that matters may be out of Cecil's control and that he may have no choice. The black intellectual finds himself in a precarious situation.

When Cecil interacts with community people, the reader can see that Cecil avoids black people because they harass, ostracize, and humiliate him and also that Cecil invites harassment with his aloofness and pretentiousness. Cecil travels through the black community on the way to the barbershop. A black shoeshine boy sets Cecil up for attack by a black crowd by offering him a free shine and then accusing Cecil of not paying.

So there was the mag[istrate] soft talking and trying to move down the street with all them niggers crowded round him. Close as white on rice. He was like a stick being carried away by the gutter or a leaf in the wind. Kinda in a daze it seemed to me I don't mind saying I felt sorry for the cat. Afterall he come to grief just trying to do some of the things most of us would do if we could get together the right shit at the right time. Who wouldn't like to walk through this jungle with his nose high like he couldn't smell the scum and even if the filth could rise up to his nose his nose held so proud and holy it couldn't be touched or hurt. Always that piece of suit and some kind of rag tie you could tell Cecil thought something of hisself and wanted to make something of hisself. The way he talked when he would talk. A book caught in his throat or a spoon shoved up his ass he dropped each word like an egg that hurt him to lose and like if he didn't get it out just right it might crack and be yolk all over the front of his shirt. He did keep a clean shirt. Holey and frayed but Esther did keep the nigger clean. Everybody knows what a fool that woman is. Thinks she got a good thing, she thinks when his day comes he's gonna be a big man and all her slaving and saving pussy just for him will pay off with loads of gravy and goodies ever after. Too bad that child don't know magistrate Cecil will drop her yellow ass quick as he gets the chance. Same old story every time. Some good woman hauls a cat up, kills herself doing his dirt, then one day he says goodbye, goodluck, I got a younger, sprier, prettier hen. But getting back to what I was saying, off they went with Cecil in the middle leaving that shoeshine boy singing on the corner.

—Never seen a fool like that. Like I'm out here for my health. Free. Did that nigger say I said free shine. In the boy's fist a quarter from the hand of Big Tony from the pants pocket of Cecil from the vest pocket of Henry Gitenstein, thirty-fifth in his class at the university law school.

Wideman has associated this scene with the Passion and has called Cecil a black Christ figure "crucified by his own people" (O'Brien 1973:221–22), but the passage also clearly leaves open the possibility that Cecil himself may be at fault. The crowd of blacks is certainly narrow-minded, insensitive, and vindictive, and we can see why Cecil needs to raise himself above its level. But on the other hand, Cecil is a pompous fool who elicits the crowd's wrath by pretending to be better than his fellow blacks in the community.

The preceding passage also shows how Wideman's use of language in *Home* moves him only very slightly closer to the attainment of a black literary voice. The passage is an infrequent place where the narrative moves outside Cecil's mind and presents the speech of a black man from the community. Black word usage, phrases, idioms, and ungrammatical, elliptical language constructions in this specific, isolated passage create a speech context that is more authentically black and reflect more genuine feeling for the black community than most of the language in *Glance.* But in depth and consistency of language structure, this passage is weak by comparison with *The Lynchers,* which follows *Home.*

Immediately at the beginning of section 2, after the scene in which the black crowd harasses Cecil at the end of section 1, Cecil tries to escape from his blackness by leaving America and the black American community and going on a European journey. Cecil undertakes his journey to Europe because, he says, he has "so little past I know of" and because he dreads "the mystery of my own past" (50–51). As we are told in the second part, Cecil does have historical knowledge of his Afro-American past: he does know his own past. Furthermore, he has a very concrete Afro-American present, as we discover at the end of section 1. As far as the text informs us, Cecil grew up in a black community and has been part of one all his life. Cecil has a historical past, which he thinks about several times in the second part, and he has lived physically in an Afro-American present which grows out of that past. Although Cecil's fantasies often contradict him, he really seems to be saying that his Afro-American reality is a mystery to him. He plainly wants to escape his Afro-American reality, and the European journey enables him to do so.

But the European journey, instead of freeing Cecil from the struggle and agony of his black American experience, produces greater pain, confusion, turmoil, and uncertainty. When Cecil denies knowledge of his Afro-American heritage—when he says that he has no personal history as a black man and is not aware of a black racial history—he is showing his confusion. But although Cecil may not always be in control and may not always be clear about what he is thinking and saying, almost everything he says and does in sections 1 and 2 indicates that he is unconsciously, if not consciously, trying to deny blackness. The journey offers a case in point. Cecil's confusion manifests itself in some of his fantasies, which entail an Afro-American legacy and thereby ironically require him to maintain an Afro-American connection. Furthermore, if Cecil needs to escape from the burden and agony of Afro-American experience, then the European trip should afford him relief and freedom, but Cecil's fantasies in Europe bespeak an even greater burden, agony, and suffering.

The subsequent fantasy about the Middle Passage and slavery has the quality of a nightmare in Cecil's mind and serves as a reminder that black reality will pursue Cecil and will torment him even more than it did when he was in the black American community. This Afro-American historical legacy is the one about which Cecil most often fantasizes. Cecil tries to convince himself that this is only "black crap inside [me]" (64), but he cannot rid himself of knowledge of this historical past. Cecil carries with him this Afro-American historical reality, which he shares with other blacks, and through it he maintains a connection with other blacks.

Another prominent fantasy in which Cecil engages relates to the painting by Hieronymus Bosch that he sees at the Prado.

The "Garden of Delights." I am a horseman in the enchanted circle. Others ride beasts magically corresponding to their species of damnation. Leopards, lions, camels, oxen, bears, hogs, deer, unnameable eclectic mounts, haunches of bloodhound, head, chest, and forelegs of an eagle, pelicans on a goat's narrow back, mounts and mounted leisurely around a charmed circle in whose center a still pool with naked women standing thigh deep in dark liquid. Black and white women their slim bodies exposed in provocative poses to the circling riders. Surface of pool broken by hands and arms of couples who copulate submerged like frogs. But the riders are barely aware of the pool and women. Some are burdened with monstrous, outsize fish, others are aroused by the closeness of nude male flesh, the sensuality of the beasts they ride or some narcissistic game they can play with touch, smell, taste, feel, and sound of themselves. Birds hop, perch, ride, fly, hover, drink, eat, sing, and screech within the scene. It could be the procession toward the ark in its profusion, its universality, yet that image modified perversely so the pageant of life projects its greediness and absurdity rather than an orderly, calm progress toward salvation. Men and beasts in an arbitrary hierarchy, even an arbitrary stability of form amuse themselves as best they can within the closed circle of the sensual dream. [51]

To Cecil, the painting becomes an inspiration for a fantasy that projects an absurd, horrific view of life and colors a lot of his thinking in section 2 of *Home.* Significantly, for Cecil the profuse, universal image is "modified perversely" so that life is greedy and absurd. This horrible fantasy world that Cecil creates around the painting suggests that he carries horror and agony in his mind, and his escape from black American reality seems only to aggravate his problem. Later, an El Greco painting works on Cecil in a similar way.

Cecil's relationship with the white prostitute Estrella also becomes a nightmarish dream-fantasy.

Each day Cecil had promised himself he would not go to Estrella, but at some point during the night he would find himself in a taxi rushing to her. Once in a drunken dream he had mounted her, ripped the sore of her from within his bowels, heaved up his rage and need in one humiliating assault after another upon her flesh. He had awakened sweating and impotent in her bed to the reality of her laughter and her fingers kneading the dough of his sex. [72]

Ironically, this connection with whiteness achieved through Estrella, which Cecil clearly implied that he wanted when he tried to escape from blackness, only intensifies the pain and suffering he felt in section 1, which he attributed to his being black. In his confusion, Cecil masochistically subjects himself again and again to the pain and horror of Estrella's world. One night Cecil sat alone, wordless for three hours in the room with Estrella's senile, almost blind mother, who broke the stillness only with an occasional belch. Except for this belch, "Cecil could have been in a room with a corpse" (72). After Estrella arrives with a sailor, Cecil stays while the old woman snores and the sounds of sex come from Estrella's room.

Cecil's other dominant fantasy in the second part has to do with being El Moro, the Moorish conqueror of Spain. "El Moro had come to town to laugh to drink and fuck and forget. At home an uppity nigger, thinks he's smart, all dressed up, Magistrate Cecil parading down the street like he owns it. But here, El Moro. Whatever else they think about the dark foreigner, they remember in their blood that he once had the upper hand, that they paid him the conqueror's tribute, that he was a teacher." (64).

In identifying with El Moro, Cecil is affirming a connection with blackness at a time when, paradoxically, he is trying to break away from it. The Moorish context places the fantasy at a greater remove from the Afro-American experience and distances the kind of pain and horror Cecil finds in his fantasy about the Middle Passage and slavery, but the identification with El Moro shows that Cecil still carries blackness within him and needs to accept it even as he runs from it.

Cecil's African journey further highlights his confusion and uncertainty and his ambivalence about blackness. At the end of the second part, Cecil journeys to Africa, where, before foreign invasion, "I rode a white horse, my beard was thick and my sword studded with jewels. Then I was a doctor; I looked to the stars and learned all manner of things of mind and body" (114). The few critics who have written about *Home* regard the African journey as an actual trip (Frazier 1975:34; Marcus 1986:322). But I think that the African journey is imaginary rather than real, another one of Cecil's fantasies; the account of this journey, after all, is quite brief. But whether the trip is real or imaginary, the main point is that Cecil, at the end of section 2, after having left his black American community to take solace in Europe's whiteness, finds at least the psychological need to travel to Africa and immerse himself in its blackness.

In discussing section 2, I have thus far focused largely on the ways in which Cecil exposes his uncertainty and confusion about his alienation from the black community and what he should do about it; also, in section 2 the narrative deals with the other characters who live in fantasy worlds that isolate them from others. These characters include Charles Webb, Al, Cecil's wife, Esther, and her Aunt Fanny.

The theme of self-isolation and alienation connects Cecil with these other characters. The narrative takes an ambivalent stance toward these characters and their thoughts and actions just as it does toward Cecil. One such character is Charles Webb, a white writer-intellectual whom Cecil meets in Spain. Webb becomes lost and confused in the fantasy of his relationship with his former black mistress Anna and his black son Charles, for whom he tries to make Cecil a surrogate. Webb's fantasy is written in words; he loses himself and Anna when he writes.

> The red notebook had begun as fragments, and its shapelessness had frightened Webb. It had been too real. Knowing Anna, knowing himself

equal impossibilities. So what could the words do but mirror inadequacy. First the red notebook had contained only his words, but later with an ocean between them, it had gradually been filled with Anna's letters, his answers sent and unsent, his impressionistic snatches of verse. Webb remembered how seldom he had reread the pages after they were covered with his words. Fear again. Anna lost somewhere in the words, himself smothered. [88]

Webb has created two black notebooks and a red notebook to use in defining reality, but clearly he is unable to define it. Webb's failed creation of Anna is a modernist fantasy and not a postmodernist fiction, because Webb, like Cecil earlier, is seeking more than subjective fulfillment; he actually wants to define and control reality through his words. Wideman is drawing directly on the black, red, yellow, and blue notebook structure of Doris Lessing's *The Golden Notebook*, where, again, words fail to capture the reality of the characters (including one named Anna).

The narrative offers little explicit information about Webb, but clearly his isolation in fantasy reflects both his experience and his uncertainty and ambivalence. Since nothing in the narrative viewpoint says otherwise, Webb, although a confused and uncertain man, may be taking the necessary steps to keep himself going, given his failed relationship with Anna and their son, whom he will apparently never see again.

The narrative expresses the same ambivalence about Al, Esther, and Fanny. Al lives the fantasy life of an adventurer, although *Home* shows that he is really a con artist. His current con game involves pretending to help Webb find his son, Charles, whom Al knows Webb will never find, while Al compels Webb to support him. Al's adventurer fantasy is self-deception, and he also deceives Webb about the con game. Moreover, Al is only supplying Webb with an illusion he needs while in the process helping himself. Al is apparently unable to do without his imaginary world and his schemes.

Esther is an even better example of a character who lives with a self-deceiving but necessary fantasy. The third section of *Home* begins with an inside portrayal of Esther and her feelings about her relationship with Cecil. Esther sees the relationship in which Cecil abuses, lies to, and deserts her in the context of her deep religious conviction. God has made Cecil her savior, the instrument of her dedication to God: Cecil "snatched [Esther] . . . from the brink of perdition" (129–30). In this context, Cecil's abuse, lying, and desertion mean nothing: to Esther, Cecil is the saint who delivers her.

Esther's world is certainly marked by isolation, confusion, and delusion, but Esther seems to have little choice. Esther, like Cecil, lives largely outside the black community because her relationship with Cecil stigmatizes her in that community. For this reason she certainly needs a sustaining place of fantasy and illusion such as the one she has created. Furthermore, to tolerate Cecil's abuse, although it may be unintentional, she needs a sustaining, protective world.

Home's narrative viewpoint toward Esther's confused, escapist fantasy world may be more sympathetic than ambivalent, and the same is true for Esther's Aunt Fanny, who lives in a fantasy world reflecting a time many years past, when her husband and sons were alive and they were all happy and living in the country. Fanny has clearly fled reality to live in her own world of fantasy and illusion, but Fanny is an old woman to whom nobody pays attention. Certainly she needs her imaginary world. Esther's and Fanny's fantasy worlds offer the best available solutions to their problems, albeit unsatisfactory ones.

In discussing these other characters who, like Cecil, live in escapist fantasy worlds without being black intellectuals alienating themselves from the black community I mean to show that the narrative takes an ambivalent stance, and where Esther and Fanny are concerned probably expresses sympathy, toward characters who escape from reality or who alienate themselves from others in fantasy worlds. This collective viewpoint of ambivalence toward the characters, who are also in some ways like Cecil, gives added weight to the ambivalence and uncertainty that the narrative viewpoint already shows toward Cecil.

Home's paradox emerges more clearly at the end of section 2 and the beginning of section 3. Cecil is plainly confused and uncertain about what he is doing. He runs from the black American community and the black experience, which he sees as painful and confining, but his fantasies reveal ties with blackness even as he seeks to sever the connection, and he finds greater horror, pain, and agony in freedom from the community than he felt within it. Furthermore, by its viewpoint the narrative implicitly criticizes Cecil and the other characters for living in their confused fantasy worlds while at the same time suggesting that they may be living in the only way they know how. Cecil may be capable of nothing better, given his intellectual experience and the disposition of the black community.

After the short focus on Esther at the beginning of section 3, *Home*'s paradox develops further over roughly the next fifty pages through Cecil's confusion and ambivalence and the narrative's ambivalence as depicted through Cecil's "journal." This large part of the third section is a journal because it depicts almost purely Cecil's thoughts—the depths of his imagination—as a journal might. Cecil explains the point himself. "There is no novel. I have a vivid imagination, and countless frustrations. Therefore I retreat to illusion, fantasy. Call my imagining my novels. Journal as close as I get. But not even journal, more like . . . like nothing but fantasy, illusion" (154). Cecil is now consciously finding his fantasies shaky and unreliable, and his acknowledgment that they are so further attests to his confusion and his seemingly ambivalent, contradictory attitude about himself. Wideman's reliance on the journal form at the end of *Home* emphasizes Cecil's instability and precarious position and supplements the narrative's ambivalence. Here Wideman is drawing directly on white modernist writers, some of whom have often used the journal form to suggest the instability and precarious states of their characters. Two examples are Lessing in *The Golden Notebook* and Joyce at the end of *A Portrait of the Artist as a Young Man*.

On the previous page, Cecil has again called attention to the chief cause of his retreat into the world of fantasy and illusion. This is his frustration with living in the day-to-day world with other black people.

Cecil Otis Braithwaite. First of his race to do, to be, etc. You proved something, Cecil. You are in fact the only one of your race. There is only one black man in the world. Love him. He has no brothers, no look alikes, not even dogs to be loved in the bargain. Just say *I repent.* Just say *I forswear all rights and privileges.* Just say *they* [other Black people] *are not real.* Real is Cecil, real were those fine white men your classmates and what they do and what you will do as practitioner of the law. Nothing good comes without sacrifice. Christ paid for our sins. Let *them* [other Black people] pay for their own. Don't you know they'll only drag you down, eat you up, Cecil. Being one of *them* is as impossible, frankly, as is being one of us [white people]. That's fact, it's written. I kid you not. Just look at the realities of the situation. Whose sins do you care to die for? [153]

Cecil goes on to tell himself that he need not die for black people's sins, since, through his own choice, he can make them unreal.

In tone the quoted passage is similar to the ironically critical part of the first section in which Cecil looks in the mirror and wants to eliminate his blackness. Cecil's assertive attitude in the face of the rejection of black people stands in opposition to the disparagement of himself in the passage preceding this one, where he speaks of his journal. The two sections present a contrast and another example of the confusion and ambivalence that build into paradox.

The journal continues with an account of Cecil's escape into a confused fantasy world to avoid the black community. After Cecil returns from his European journey, there is a long account of a time he spends in Constance Beauty's hair salon–barbershop. (Critics who have mentioned this episode—Frazier, 1975:35, Marcus 1986:322— assert that Cecil is working in the salon. According to my reading of the text, this point is not clear.) Cecil is physically in the middle of the black community but plays a word game that enables him to distance himself psychologically and imaginatively from the people and events. The surrealistic description of Walt Willis's head locks Cecil firmly in his own fantasy world.

And this is Walter Willis' head, before and after. Quite a difference, eh. Like between being seen in a Cadillac or in a Ford. How many pimps you know drive Fords.

 . . . and this is Walter Willis, first potato of the day dropping in the bubbling fat. Let me advise you of something Walt. These hands about to be violently laid on your head are the hands of a man who has scaled Mendelian ladders time out of mind from tiniest spoor of salty rot past sloths and killer apes past pithecanthropus and your Neanderthal experiment. Walter I have highwayed my way straight and narrow to this last whining spiraling exhausted dead end. Like those anthropoids that dropped from the trees too soon and could not learn the reptilian lore. Swallowed as the earth bathed in fire and ice. No canines, Walt. They had to chew and grind all day to survive. Daisy eaters, pansy eaters, eaters of the rose, daffodils, lilacs. They drink no blood, Walt, had no wine no Tiger Rose Thunderbird Pio Manischevitz Gallo Virginia Dare grapes and so they salvaged nothing from their dispossession only when they were dying did the high flying days return, vestigial, blurred, nostalgia as being devoured, a predator relieving the hot secrets of its bowels, glazed monkey eyes of the victim on his back last thing being seen as thick trees swaying, swaying through a mist. [155–56]

In the barbershop Cecil finds it difficult to disregard the black community's reality, but at the end of the barbershop section, he remains insulated from the blacks around him. The same paradox is working here. Cecil is isolating himself from the black community because he thinks he must, but he should move outside himself and contact others, because his surrealistic fantasy indicates that he is moving further into an intellectual world where he loses touch with everyone.

Earlier Cecil explained that his quest in *Home* lacked the consistency of a novel, more greatly resembled a journal, and ultimately represented illusion and fantasy. Later, Cecil returns to this idea of himself as a creator who tries to shape a clear, firm, consistent story but fails.

> Since the artist can only call the process of creation itself uniquely, truly his own in a manner that not even the finished, public manifestation of that process is his own, the most pure art and the one perhaps most satisfying would be the most ephemeral art, the art that was all process, all unfolding, all experience, the art which removed the necessity of an exportable, finished process. . . . The possibilities [of creation] were endless and the challenges a limitation not of the medium but of the imagination of the challenger. [160]

Cecil also speaks of this process as a "word game" and refers to his inability "to make a rounded, full tale I have never lived through, nor anyone lives through" (168–69).

Cecil persists in the creation of fantasies that leave his existence open and commit him to nothing; he is no longer even committed to whiteness, as he was earlier. Cecil was ambivalent about this stance in the passage where he specifically spoke of his fantasy and illusion, but he finally accepts its validity. Cecil now finds himself in a different realm of abstraction. He appears to be falling into a void between blackness and whiteness, a situation more dangerous than his escape from the black world into the white.

Cecil becomes more fragmented and disjointed as the journal progresses. In the process he becomes more like Joyce's young artist in *Portrait*, who at the end of *Portrait* shows the effects of his ordeal in the Irish crucible of isolation and alienation. The concluding section of the journal is a dialogue between Cecil and his Uncle Otis, who resembles Cecil's alter ego more than an actual person. This is the most abstract, deeply imaginative section of *Home*, and it plunges more deeply than any other section into Cecil's disjointed psyche.

By talking to his alter ego, however, Cecil appears to be searching for a clearer, firmer position. He tries to explain why he left Esther and went off with Webb and why he has played with reality. Cecil is attempting to reach a resolution: have his deeds been all right, and what is he going to do now? In the end Cecil takes the advice of his alter ego, which is given in a strange, abstruse section of *Home*.

> I once knew a dwarf. Well not exactly a dwarf, but a child who was not really a child but an old man who had grown up too fast, in a matter of months from twelve to fifty then died of old age right there in bed. He said they called it progeria, growing up too fast, all life passes like a film at the wrong speed, days are hours, months, days, a year might stretch to a week. His mind was storm but some days there was calm, he could talk a moment. I lost my job at the hospital because I did nothing but hang around at his bedside waiting for the lucid minutes. His voice would come from far away, a man's voice from the wrinkled old, new bundle of flesh he had become. [180]

The way in which Cecil's alter ego speaks to him in this weird, surreal fantasy reveals much about the state of Cecil's mind; it reveals a psyche that is disjointed and out of rhythm. But as the quotation proceeds, it also affirms Cecil in his world of isolation and illusion.

He said:

> —*In me all things occur with unbearable intensity. Never a pause for my emotions to rest, for some experience of my blood's growth to become quiet and calm before the next tumult begins. My whole being races, is scourged by time. Always losing and dying without even the illusion of possession. I cry because I cannot have this illusion, because it is an illusion, a nothing, and yet you are blessed because you have this nothing. I cry for an illusion, for a lie to deceive me. I cry because I must tell myself this lie would be better than my body's truth. I cry because I am not made to live the lie.*
>
> I didn't dream this dwarf man, neither his clenched baby fists nor the choked, panting of his voice when he spoke. He wearied me nephew. I grew tired watching him die so quickly, just as your hurrying makes me lose my breath. Go, go to her [Esther] and the rest. You see me here, where I have been, what I brought back and what I have. They laugh at me and they'll laugh at you. They see in us only themselves, and because they are what they are, can only laugh at themselves. I kissed the dwarf when he slept hoping I would be infected. [180–81]

Cecil ventures far into abstraction here, but he seems to be telling himself that his escape into a world of illusion is good for him. Once again Cecil's illusions give him something that allows him to survive his experience with the black community and to remain a black intellectual. Cecil's ambivalence and the narrative's ambivalent stance persist to the end. The discouraging paradox remains. Cecil is saved at the end of *Home*, but because of the paradox his existence remains precarious.

Cecil returns to Esther after three years. There seems to be a moonlight magic in the room as Esther lies sleeping. An aura of the demonic magic of *Walpurgisnacht* is present, and a "harsh theatrical moonlight framed by the narrow window [made] all things [seem] possible" (184–85). By returning to Esther and accepting "his darkness, his room" and the aura just described, Cecil would seem to be accepting the fantasies, illusions, and lies that, according to Uncle Otis, make life meaningful. In so doing, Cecil, unlike the dwarf, will not have to "cry because I am not made to live the lie." Cecil makes a final peace with his world of fantasy and illusion at this time. He has done the good, responsible thing by returning to Esther, but he will continue to live in his fantasy world. (The last three words of *Home* are: "So Cecil dreamed.")

In *Home*, Wideman vividly and effectively renders Cecil's escape into fantasy by means of mainstream modernist techniques. One of Wideman's techniques, as I have noted, is what we would call traditionally stream of consciousness, but he uses others as well. He plays on words, develops appropriate surreal descriptions and images, and produces recondite references to suggest Cecil's inner feelings and often horrific mental states and to project his self-willed transformation and transcendence of the world outside him.

The following short passage shows Wideman playing on words in an attempt to depict Cecil's comic-serious mental state. "Little light on the whorizon. Silent distance. I will walk toward that myth of earth touching heaven as good a destination as any I can perceive, as any revealed to Cecil in the last consultation of his whoroscope" (109). Wideman is showing Cecil's mental state as he prepares to leave Estrella. The play on the word "whore" ("whorizon" and "whoroscope") makes Cecil's feeling about this prostitute partly comic, but the rest of the passage quoted and the larger context here demonstrate that the departure from Estrella is serious because he has grown to depend on her so much. This specific use of wordplay resembles Joyce's technique in *Ulysses* (Frazier 1975:31). But the use of the word "whoroscope" clearly recalls Samuel Beckett's poem with that title, and the wit and style of the puns in "Whoroscope" (Gluck 1979:44–45) color Wideman's pun on the word "whore."

Wideman creates the modernist horrific mental states that Cecil ironically encounters as he escapes the unpleasant black experience. When Cecil has the nightmare in Estrella's bed, for example, the description of Cecil's rage and impotence is surreal: "he had mounted her, ripped the sore of her from within his bowels, heaved up his rage and need in one humiliating assault after another upon her flesh. He awakened sweating and impotent . . . to the reality of her laughter and her fingers kneading the dough of his sex."

Wideman uses images, together with references to Cecil's interest in the creative power of words, as a way of showing his great psychological need to transcend the world outside himself. Examples appear in an earlier passage where Wideman creates the talking mirror ("Mirror said time was Cecil when you could not see your face unless someone lifted you to the broken glass above the sink") and says that the "Word" is "become flesh become Cecil become invisible opener of doors."

The narration in the journal is often fragmented and disconnected. In effect it approaches the actual movement of thought in the mind under stress, which is slightly reminiscent of Faulkner in *The Sound and the Fury*, for example, when he uses the stream-of-consciousness technique.

> You see
> In the mirror
> Returning do I create a mind looking back. You have a white T-shirt just like mine. Do you sleep in it always.
> Hair grows after death. As do fingernails. Even after death to be shaved, manicured, pedicured as if something still depended on the living as if it does now. I have been tempted to grow a prophet's beard, to forsake soap and water. I am a cliché unto myself. Saying, doing the same things, the blood things I can disguise but not change. What was never thought and only poorly expressed. Sum of being. Another said when it's poetry you cut yourself if thinking of it and shaving. OOO you Shagspearean rug cuddled round my chin. The storm, the hot gates, cold steel, warm steel, steel too hot *señor* you are about to burn. [144–45]

It seems clear that Cecil is reflecting on human existence and reality and is wittily philosophizing (using literary allusions to Eliot and Joyce), but part of the narrative also goes deep into Cecil's inner consciousness, where his meaning and frame of reference are private and not totally accessible to the reader. The associations ("Another said when it's poetry you cut yourself if thinking of it and shaving," for example) are not fully intelligible. This is the landscape of Cecil's disjointed mind, and Wideman depicts this mind in crisis.

Wideman's portrayal of Cecil in *Home* allows him to depict a wider range of black life in *The Lynchers*, where he uses mainstream modernist techniques and forms in conjunction with a more thorough treatment of black life. Wideman moves closer to achieving a black voicing of modernist concerns in *Lynchers*.

The Lynchers

A Destructive Community, a Failed Quest, and an Incipient Voice

In *The Lynchers* (1973), the last of the early books, Wideman
portrays black intellectuals who differ in orientation from Cecil in
Home. Overall, the intellectuals are not as much products of formal
Western training and do not make this training a central reference
point in their lives. They strive to be leaders and activists on the
streets of the black community and want to be a part of that
community. Like Cecil, however, in the end they isolate themselves
from the community to a significant extent because the community
is not capable of accepting their contribution. Littleman, Wideman's
main leader-activist character in *Lynchers*, lacks Cecil's formal
Western education, but he is an intellectual by virtue of his superior
intelligence and his leadership and activism, which are as much
rooted in the mind's deep, abstruse workings as Cecil's escapism is.
Another of Wideman's characters, Thomas Wilkerson, has more

formal education and is less of a deep thinker, but he still distinguishes himself as an intellectual because his actions develop from a process of careful, close consideration of ideas that most people do not pursue.

The characters' attempt to be a part of the community shows that Wideman has moved toward a view that the black intellectual should definitely play a role in the black community; the intellectuals' eventual alienation from the community and destruction in *Lynchers* show that Wideman sees no possible place for them, to a significant extent because of the poor, oppressed state of the community. Comparison of *Lynchers* with *Glance* and *Home* shows that Wideman's conception of the intellectual's identity and role has broadened, but his conclusion about his relationship to the community remains the same.

Lynchers is Wideman's first book to be set entirely in the black community and to give an important place in its structure to black historical tradition, speech, and cultural tradition. Wideman still does not achieve the full, mature black voice that we find in the Homewood trilogy, however. His acute sense of oppressive black historical tradition, his skillful rendition of black speech, and his portrayal of black rituals, together with his use of modernist surreal form, stream-of-consciousness technique, and thematic pessimism certainly move him closer to the full, mature voicing of common black and modernist concerns that he achieved in the Homewood trilogy. But when he wrote *Lynchers*, Wideman was not knowledgeable enough about the workings of black tradition to achieve this full, mature black voice. Later, when Wideman had informed himself about the richness and substance of black culture, had distanced the mainstream modernist concept of the alienated artist-intellectual, and had himself moved closer to the black community, he strengthened his black voice, made it dominant over the mainstream modernist voice, and integrated the black intellectual into the substantive black culture and community of which he had become aware. Only after he had read black writers extensively and had himself participated in the black community could he do so. *The Lynchers* is clearly a pivotal book at the end of the early stage; it paves the way for Wideman's achievement in the Homewood trilogy.

Lynchers presents paradoxes that recall those in *Home.* Black community participation is fulfilling for the black intellectual because he is carrying out a necessary role, but it is also harmful because it alienates him from the community and destroys him. The black intellectual would be secure if he sequestered himself from the black community, but he cannot comfortably do so because his most important role lies in helping the community. Wideman works himself into paradoxes that it will take him eight years (the time between *Lynchers* and *Hiding Place*) to escape, but these paradoxes produce brilliant fiction in *Lynchers*.

Wideman described *Lynchers* in the following way.

> *The Lynchers* is . . . in a very realistic tradition. I have learned from the nonrepresentational school about fantasy and playing around with different forms. The novel started out with these two tendencies—realism and fantasy. *The Lynchers* is in part plot-oriented; I wanted to create drama and get the reader involved with it. On the other hand, the subject of the book is imagination. The novel absorbs some of the philosophical assumptions that caused experiments in form over the last several years, and attempts to merge them with a more traditional plot-line. [O'Brien 1973:217]

This statement from Wideman, among other things, identifies an emphasis on dramatic, external plot events in *The Lynchers* that is not present in *Home*. Wideman describes a series of historical events well and portrays the characters, all of whom are black, as trying to keep abreast of events in the external black community.

Even more important than the emphasis on plot itself is the characters' strong desire to keep in contact with and help other black people; the characters are willing and try, but on the most important thematic level, they cannot escape their imaginations to reverse the harmful traditions of the black community. The characters can do things that perpetuate the black community's destructive traditions, but Thomas Wilkerson and Littleman cannot bring their plan out of their imaginations to affect progressive political change in the black community, which would be the most important thing in the book.

At the beginning of *Lynchers*, Wideman presents what he calls the "Matter Prefatory," which he felt readers would have to accept as real events before the book's "imaginative world" could stand as linked to oppressive black history (O'Brien 1973:218). The "Matter Prefatory" becomes an important part of the book's historical plot and drama and the major source for some of the characters' imaginings. It presents an account of white racist thinking and atrocities committed against blacks from several historical sources, including B. A. Botkin's *Lay My Burden Down* and Herbert Aptheker's *A*

Documentary History of the Negro People in the United States.
White voices tell of the need to keep blacks oppressed in their
subordinate place; black voices tell of the heinous acts perpetrated
and cry out for relief. Because the accounts in the "Matter Prefatory"
so poignantly reveal the brutal, ruthless toll that racism has taken
on black life, anyone reading them and knowing that racism persists
would be unlikely to think, like Cecil, that a black person could
retreat to a world of fantasy insulated from the legacy of black
oppression.

The "Matter Prefatory" is a crucial structural feature of *Lynchers*
because it very forcefully supports a worldview that sets a high
priority on attention to the black community and on activism as a
remedy for the problems in that community. It clearly implies that
black individuals need to play some kind of activist role in their
community, even if they merely identify with it and interact with
its members. When one considers the cold-blooded truth of the
actual historical accounts presented in the "Matter Prefatory" and
the strong connections between these accounts and events in the
black present, then the fanciful imaginary journey, largely detached
from action in the external black world, that Cecil takes in *Home*
becomes unlikely.

Black speech and black music, two unique and important aspects
of the black community, form an important part of Wideman's
developing black voice, which tempers his mainstream modernist
voice; in the novel, knowledge of black speech and music defines
the characters' place and participation in the community. The
characters in *Lynchers* know black music and use black speech.
Orin Wilkerson (Sweetman), for example, can sing gospel songs and
shows a real appreciation for jazz, and the speech of the characters
throughout *Lynchers* demonstrates that Wideman understands black
speech on an intimate level that he did not demonstrate in either
Glance or *Home.* The characters speak in the rhythms and use the
vivid, colorful figures of black speech. Their statements range in
style from vulgar, blunt street talk to a kind of elegance that stems
from the ready assimilation of formally correct phrases into the
rhythm of black speech and into the black worldview.

The narrator at one point describes the range of Leonard Saunders's language when he is at the hospital, where he is visiting Willie
Hall (Littleman), whom the police beat after he made a speech at a
demonstration.

—Pigs usually swing that rubber hose with more circumspection. Don't like to leave marks. *Circumspection*. The word incongruous in Saunders' speech, a loose end like his spotless underwear. Wasn't simply ostentation. Words such as circumspection frequently laced his conversation. Employed always with accuracy, a sense of verbal nuance, but simultaneously mocking the words and himself as he used them. He communicated his awareness of a larger picture, the sense of irony he felt at being trapped in a language whose formal modes excluded him. When he said circumspection he was playing an intricate game, reverse slumming, burying black dogs at night in the white only section of a cemetery. [Wideman 1973:139–40]

Saunders, a skillful user of language, knows that Littleman will understand the use of the formal word "circumspection" and will appreciate the verbal dexterity with which he uses it and the ironic, mocking tone as well. They both know that they are part of a black community which borrows the tools of language from a dominant culture, must get a certain aesthetic pleasure from the use of these tools, and must at the same time appropriate them to mock the oppression that made it necessary to use them in the first place.

The traditional black practice of ritualizing language to achieve results magically in daily life is not nearly as important or clearly articulated in *Lynchers* as in *Hiding Place* and *Damballah*; however, the correct and precise use of words, which is similar to language ritualization for magical effect in *Hiding Place* and *Damballah*, is important in the characters' attempts to make the plan a political reality. The characters strive for a magical relationship between words and reality just as Cecil does in *Home*, but these characters think differently from Cecil because, by magically and imaginatively using words, they are trying to create political change in the black community, while Cecil was trying to escape the black community. Thomas Wilkerson believes that it will take the right words to bring about the desired political act of publicly lynching a white policeman. "The wrong words would contaminate everything. . . . the deed did have some magic relationship to the words. That was why Littleman was angry in the park, why he became pedantic in his references to what they were doing. What they said they were doing was what the act would be. It had to be precise, it had to be *lynching a white cop*" (60).

Littleman, the leader of the conspiracy to lynch a white cop, tries to use words to bring about a political upheaval. Thomas feels both repelled and attracted by Littleman's words, but he cannot shake off the fear of the consequences of the political act that the words magically create. "The shower of words passed. Real or unreal, outside or inside it drenched him and shivers twitched from head to toe till nothing remained but the cold night and Thomas Wilkerson" (67–68).

Other, more mainstream modernist devices than black language uses reflect the characters' attempts to have an impact on the external world of the black community. Thomas's dreams, for example, reflect on his repulsion from and attraction to the political act of lynching the white cop and his own worthiness as a person capable of taking significant action in the black community. Throughout *Lynchers*, the characters' dreams, as well as their words, reflect on the political lynching and their worth as political beings in the external world of the black community.

In the last passage quoted, Thomas is right to fear the consequences of words. The black characters' words can magically create a trap for them, because their words do make real a political upheaval and its consequences in each other's imaginations and for this reason can affect their interactions among themselves. But the heavy reliance on words and dreams to project reality beyond the imagination and change the black community through revolutionary violence seems misguided. These characters (especially Thomas) have some sense that it is, because they question themselves, and certainly Wideman raises questions about them by making it clear how weak words and dreams are as resources to bring about a violent revolution that will liberate the black community. But at the same time, they are noble to attempt the necessary job of alleviating oppressive conditions in the community. The paradoxes that are central in *Lynchers* are similar to those in *Home*.

The strategy of bringing about societal upheaval by lynching a white policeman—the plan, which Thomas believes must be magically structured in exactly the right words—is a symbolic action that will reverse black and white realities and change history. It will reverse, or at least stop, the oppressive historical pattern documented in the "Matter Prefatory." In broad daylight in the middle of the black community, the four black conspirators—Thomas Wilkerson, Littleman, Leonard Saunders, and Graham Rice—will instigate the lynching of a white policeman, who will have a sack of flour poured over him as members of the black community stand and watch. The conspirators will kill a black prostitute who is hustling for the policeman and will frame the policeman as the killer. The policeman's manipulation and the murder of the prostitute will symbolize the wide range of atrocities that whites have committed against blacks. But even more important, the spectacle of the policeman will galvanize the collective will of the black masses, who will participate in his lynching and will thereby inform whites of their intention to be recognized as equals or to die in violent, revolutionary warfare. The act will show that blacks have as much power as whites and that they will now begin to assert this power to make an example of a white oppressor whenever they wish. Whites have always exercised a similar arbitrary, ruthless power over blacks; in fact, whites used such power to fashion a significant part of Afro-American history. One simple, bold, outrageous symbolic act will have the strength to change both black people and the direction of Afro-American history. Not only the words that describe the plan but the plan itself, as a totality, through its simple, imaginative genius, is magical in its ability to transform the black community so that it immediately ceases to be oppressed and becomes the militant controller of its destiny. The conspirators can never quite grasp and project the plan as a concrete action; it remains more a magical conception described in magical words.

An analysis of *Lynchers'* characters shows that they are unable to translate the plan from their artful language and their imaginations to any kind of political reality in the community. Littleman is the author of the plan, and he cannot be there on the day specified to carry it out because he has been hospitalized after a severe beating from the police. Despite the fertility of Littleman's imagination and the strength of his political rhetoric, Littleman shows no practical ability to execute the plan. The plan is supposed to be the ultimate goal for which all four men are sacrificing everything, but Littleman jeopardizes it by leading a rally at a junior high school and letting the police beat him up. Littleman never explains why he would put himself, the mastermind of the plan, in a position where he would be unable to supervise it when the time came.

But there are several other examples of Littleman's problem in the book. Part of the difficulty is that he cannot make the plan a reality; for one thing he has trouble holding onto *any* reality in his life. As we see from other parts of *Lynchers,* he cannot convert a large part of the illusion he creates with his powerful upper body and with his words into objective reality. Furthermore, at points he cannot distinguish between external reality and the dream-fantasies of his

mind or transform these dream-fantasies to action. Once, in a bar in
Atlantic City, Littleman propositioned a prostitute as he sat in a
booth with his body half concealed, "the illusion of a whole man
since his braces trailed off into obscurity below the table." The
prostitute accepts, and when she is following Littleman outside, he
turns to find that she is laughing. "My smooth talking Papa ain't
hardly big as a minute. Kiss my ass I say then I can't hardly keep a
straight face walking behind you. . . . Game little man. Scrambling
outa there like you in a real hurry too. Into something, I guess you
thought. Well, now we out here, you can forget it. Janice ain't for no
freak tricks. Straight fucking all this girl gonna do. That's why I stay
away from them white boys" (127). Littleman insists to the prostitute that he can do the job, and agrees to pay her half the money in
advance. The prostitute takes the money and runs, flinging insults
over her shoulder: "—You telling me what a badass cocksman you
are. Well, if you so bad, catch my butt and you can have all the pussy
you want." Her final words are "Cripple freaky motherfucker," as
Littleman helplessly throws his cane after her (128).

Wideman uses Littleman's crippled body to make a statement
about the conspirators' unrealistic attempts to change the external
world of the black community. Littleman can present an illusion of
himself while he is sitting at the bar, and his smooth talk is enough
to excite a prostitute about the possibilities. But the withered legs
cannot maneuver him into position to demonstrate what he believes
is his sexual prowess.

What seems to be for Littleman a meaningful relationship with a
woman, Angela, becomes at least partly an unsatisfying dream-
fantasy. When Littleman met Angela just off the boardwalk one
summer in Atlantic City, she seemed to be a different kind of
woman, one who would appreciate his inner qualities and would not
judge him on the basis of his physical deformity. But Angela finally
terminates the relationship, and leaves Littleman waiting at their
last proposed meeting place; he never sees her again. He must
retreat into dream-fantasy to conjure up explanations for Angela's
actions, but the explanations are not satisfactory. Littleman wonders, "Who had been speaking in my dream?" and "Had I invented a
life for Angela?" He also says, "If I doubted the dream, why not
doubt the total memory of Angela; accept the interlude as fiction. . . ?" (171). Littleman clearly has a problem translating dream-
fantasy into actions that take place in the external world.

After doubting the reality of his relationship with Angela, Littleman tries to reinforce the idea of the plan as a shaper of history. "If there is orderliness, precision, cleanliness, rhythm in the world, they are most visible in an action, a plan such as I have conceived. Formulating a rite totally consistent with the logic of history, yet harnessing the blind rush of events, opening a momentary wedge so a new myth can shoulder its way into the process" (172).

Littleman may be articulate enough now, but after his demonstrated ineffectuality—with the police, with the prostitute, and with Angela—we not only do not believe in the plan, which we may have found totally illusory in the first place, but we start to doubt Littleman's ability to function effectively in the day-to-day world of the streets. He may want to be an activist, to translate his militant black power fantasies into activist political strategies, but he remains a dreamer, thoroughly out of touch with whatever black activism may actually exist in the black community.

Near the end of part 2, Littleman, as he slips in and out of a coma caused by his beating at the hands of the police, tries to indoctrinate a young black orderly named Anthony; here we finally see the beginning of Littleman's disintegration. Littleman thinks he is in control with Anthony and can manipulate him to be an instrument in carrying out the plan, but he becomes progressively more confused as he tries to use Anthony to benefit the plan. Littleman vacillates between pride in his ability to control Anthony and fear and confusion as to whether he has compromised the plan with Anthony.

At the end of part 2, Littleman is the ineffectual modernist figure as well as the intellectual alienated from the community as represented by Anthony. He totally loses control of himself. "I must have been shouting," he realizes, and the nurses and orderlies rush in to sedate him (194). The description of Littleman's death at the end of the book reinforces the idea that he is a hopelessly confused dreamer; as Littleman dies, his eyes seem "hopelessly torn from a task in his dream" (263).

Ultimately, Littleman is a thinker who is no more effective in the black community than Cecil. In the middle of Littleman's disintegration near the end of part 2, he dreams that a black god is being born. The person being born seems to be a potentially dynamic force that will affect the destiny of blacks. But the surreal modernist description of the birth takes us as deep as we go into the recesses of Littleman's mind and, at this point in *Lynchers*, emphasizes that he is hopelessly lost in dream. The dream is another part of Littleman's disintegration, and again futility is strongly evident in Wideman's mainstream modernist voice. Wideman's portrayal of Littleman leaves no doubt that the conspirators never had a chance to translate the plan from imagination to action and thus to change the black community.

Thomas Wilkerson has a different set of problems from Littleman, to a large extent because he lacks Littleman's purity of conviction, but he falls into Littleman's confusion and, like Littleman, dies before the end of the book. As I have said, Thomas is another one of Wideman's intellectuals, and his initial doubts to some extent stem from his having achieved the middle-class status of a schoolteacher. His life is comfortable and structured. His girlfriend is another teacher, an attractive, extremely poised black woman. He has what many black people want.

Dealing with other black people is exactly what Cecil tried not to do in *Home*, of course, but Wideman shows that it is the right course of action on the conspirators' part, even though they cannot translate it into revolutionary change. Throughout *Lynchers*, Thomas fights against resigning himself to the notion that his black power fantasies have no reality in the community. After the police have beaten and neutralized Littleman, Thomas wonders how he could fear Littleman's plan when the white power structure can eliminate Littleman so easily. He sees "all the Willies [Littlemen] and Sweetmen [such as Orin, his father] and shadows like himself dreaming puny dreams, alive at best in some muted fantasy under-world, lying, cheating, even killing to avoid the simple truth" (143–44). At the same time, he paradoxically refuses to accept the truth and pushes himself to make Littleman's fantasies a reality, to affirm "that something did exist even when the dreamer was awake" (146). He tells himself that action and thought are both deadly, but action is preferable because it "gets you out of a room, onto the street, bumps you into other human beings" (147).

Thomas cannot maintain his positive attitude toward action and interaction, however. His father Sweetman kills his best friend in a fight over an insignificant amount of money. The senselessness of the killing makes Thomas question the efficacy of an activist strategy such as the plan in a world where things are accidental, arbitrary, and senseless. The notion of carrying out the plan in a senseless, chaotic world leads Thomas to further analysis of the plan and two of its victims, the prostitute Sissie and her daughter, Lisa.

He needed to know about Sissie, the woman he was plotting to kill, and all the other deaths. Was killing Sissie unavoidable? Had she forfeited her life? Had Childress [his father's best friend and murder victim] forfeited his? And the Sweetman? Was everything an accident? The madman an accident, the white people, the cop? What was the limit of accident? How could you form a plan in a world where all that mattered was accidental, a blind jumble of blind forces? [213]

Thomas sees Lisa and becomes sentimental about preserving black life, with all of its poverty, degradation, and humble rituals of subsistence. Thomas goes to the dilapidated place where Sissie lives and finds Lisa sitting on the steps, singing a rhyme about a goose and a monkey who went to heaven on a billy goat's back, creating her own comforting fantasy in the midst of poverty and ruins. He realizes that someone who loved Lisa taught her the song and that Sweetman did the same thing for him. Thomas wants to shield Lisa rather than kill her. Looking at what seems to him to be the meager stuff that allows black people to survive, in this case their simplistic songs and their gospels (which his father also sang), Thomas cannot see pursuing a plan that will destroy black life in the process of attempting to enhance it.

Thomas goes to talk to his girlfriend Tanya after he sees Lisa, and at this point he reaches the depths of confusion and irresolution. Thomas talks to Tanya about the conspirators' decision to strive for change for blacks. We, he remarks, " 'decided on a way to prepare a catalyst. Stage an event so traumatically symbolic that things could never be the same afterwards. Lynch a white cop. Lynch one in broad daylight and say to white people what they have been saying to us for so long.' 'Littleman is a genius. A genius because the obvious is always clear to him' " (236). Thomas ends the conversation with Tanya, in which he seems to be talking about the correctness and necessity of the plan, by saying that he must go to Graham Rice, get the guns from him, and stop the plan. He believes that Tanya is totally wrong to call him and the plan insane, but he must still stop the plan.

Thomas becomes caught in *Lynchers'* paradoxes. He is overwhelmed by the reality of the need for him to undertake a revolutionary process that is necessary but senseless and impossible. His dream fantasies will remain in his imagination and will never affect the black community, and he will remain an ineffectual intellectual in the mainstream modernist tradition. In the night,

Rice shoots, and presumably kills, Thomas as he bangs on Rice's door and loudly whispers his name.

Leonard Saunders, one of the conspirators, does seem capable of executing the plan. Saunders's cold callousness makes him unlike any of the other conspirators: Saunders is a potential murderer, an assassin. He has almost none of Thomas's introspection and compassion and almost none of the sensitivity that Littleman is capable of showing, especially to women.

The life of the street hustler has hardened Saunders, but his problems have deeper roots: they stem from his upbringing in a broken, devastated, and scattered family of fifteen children, by various fathers, guided by a psychotic mother. Saunders listened and looked as his mother produced from her troubled mind stories and rituals that gave differing, conflicting accounts of their family history and condition. Once, while she was hotly accusing God and cursing her fate, she tore all her clothes off as Saunders watched.

> They had always called him cold. He knew why then. A numbness in his limbs, an icy wind swirling through his chest. Cold and nothing else as she frantically stripped each garment from her body. His mother stretched naked on the floor. Cold. She could have been a strange corpse on a slab rolled out from the morgue's cold storage. Her flesh so arbitrary he could have taken a scalpel, if prodded by his curiosity, and sliced down to the clockwork innards. His mother's body, female because someone had snatched something from the point of her groin and left a hairy emptiness, female because someone had taken two fistfuls of flesh and hurled them with such force against her chest that they had flattened and stuck.
>
> Spraddle legged on the floor. Last act of the family chronicle she endlessly recited to him. Termination and beginning. On her back to receive another lover, to birth another Saunders, to welcome madness and worms. Hunched over her were swarms of bulky shadows she cooed to and called by name. Her bony hips pitching. Her palms and loose backsides slapping on the gritty floor. [149]

Saunders developed a cold detachment from his mother and other people in general; Littleman has selected him for the conspirators' killer because of his coldness and meanness. In his assassin's role, Saunders calculatingly stalks Sissie and Lisa, preparing himself for the time when he will kill Sissie. When he sees Lisa, Saunders does wonder if she is his brother's daughter, as Sissie claims she is, and he does feel concern briefly and contemplates giving her one hundred dollars rather than the token amount it would take for him to enter and case Sissie's dwelling so that he could finish planning to kill her.

But Saunders brushes tenderness and sympathy aside and focuses on his task.

Saunders feels sure of himself. He believes that the plan has freed him to take significant action, but he finds himself very frustrated by the other conspirators, particularly Thomas. On the first day of the intended revolution, the first day of the plan's operation, Thomas asks Saunders to meet him at a bar, but Thomas is killed by Rice before the meeting can take place. As Saunders waits, his anger and frustration reach a high pitch. When last we see Saunders, he is resolute about carrying out the plan, but he is totally frustrated by Thomas's seemingly consistent capriciousness and irresponsibility. Like a madman, Saunders lunges to grab Thomas by the throat when the door of the bar opens, only to slide helplessly back into his booth when someone else appears at the door.

The fact that Saunders in particular would take action to make the plan a political reality is a sad thing for the conspirators and a bad sign for the black community. Only a cold, ruthless, callous man like Saunders could attempt the kind of bold action that would be significant, symbolically at least, for black people. People who are introspective and compassionate, like Thomas, or even slightly sensitive or deeply imaginative, like Littleman, are destined to be thwarted from action, to a significant extent by their positive qualities and abilities.

Wideman is saying that Saunders is not an intellectual and that intellectuals such as Littleman and Thomas, although they do not think in the traditional ways, as Cecil and Wideman himself do, must have some part in changing the black community. I do not mean that Wideman condones Littleman's violence; rather, his force and fertility of mind, together with Thomas's thoughtfulness and compassion, are important for the community. But how can they be a part of change, when being an intellectual seems to mean becoming trapped in one's imagination and becoming ineffectual or precluding action by posing paradoxical questions with regard to the overall conditions and circumstances of black people?

Wideman obviously considers black intellectuals important people who should contribute to solving problems in the black community. But he also seems to believe that the severity of the problems, the difficulty of change, and the paradoxical and varied nature of the manifestations of oppression will cause an intellectual or thinker to find himself lost or to lose himself in an inextricable web of thought and imagination. Wideman must wait for the

Homewood trilogy, where he penetrates deeper into the black community and examines it with more than a pessimistic modernist attitude, to resolve his quandary about the role of the black intellectual and thinker.

Wideman's portrayal of Graham Rice illustrates my argument. Rice is not an intellectual but a man of relatively simple mind who is a conniving flunky for the others. As in Saunders's case, Rice's intellectual capabilities and the qualities associated with them are not responsible for his failure to execute the plan. If Littleman were not dying and if Rice himself had not shot Thomas from hatred and malice, then he, like Saunders, could certainly be instrumental in making the plan a concrete reality. Saunders's ability to carry out the concrete manifestations of the plan, as Littleman and Thomas could not, is a bad sign for the black community, but it is also a bad sign that Rice could do the same thing. Rice is not as cold and mean as Saunders, but in some ways he is more crude, less inventive (and thus less attractive), and more dangerous than Saunders.

I have been focusing on the intellectuals' ineffectuality and inability to make their plan a reality, but the poor, oppressed, self-destructive condition of the black community (as embodied in Orin) clearly plays a large role in determining the intellectuals' failure. The black community presents paradoxes and unsolvable dilemmas for thinkers such as Thomas, and its powerlessness at least in part makes Littleman's deep ingenuity ludicrous and ineffective.

Especially given the places where Orin appears in the book, at the beginning of the first and last parts and very near the end, I would argue that Orin's carelessness and destructiveness present the external, day-to-day reality of the black community. Part 1 opens with a description of Orin's loose ways and horrible family life. The third and last part begins by recounting Orin's murder of his best friend, Childress. And the next to last section of part 3, a short one, shows us Orin and his wife, Bernice, pitifully wondering whether they can reach out to Childress's widow, Mamie.

The portrayal of Orin's family is a sad commentary on the terrible, destructive daily existence of the black family. Orin is not a malicious person, but his actions are devastating for himself, his family, and his friends. He still wants to love his wife, but all of his children have grown up, leaving him and Bernice alone together in a dilapidated apartment with a marriage that for years has lacked warmth and feeling. Orin's constant long flights from home and his womanizing are destroying Bernice and are making life hell on earth for both of them. The bad family atmosphere created by Orin infects Thomas as he stumbles to win Tanya and perhaps to start his own family. A nasty argument between Orin and Bernice ruins Thomas's attempt to introduce Tanya to his parents. In reality Orin and his family are not close to grasping the import of the plan. For them the plan exists in the twilight zone of the mind, where indeed it largely remains in this book.

This view of a pitiful black existence results partly from Wideman's ignorance of black culture, and from his view of the naturalistic effects of the oppressive black historical legacy, as portrayed in the "Matter Prefatory," and partly from the influence on Wideman of modernist pessimism. The view of black life held by Wideman extends beyond Orin's family to the lives of his friends and other blacks, for example, to those whom we see in the jail scenes. Orin and Childress have been friends for years, and yet they can get into a knife fight in which Childress forces Orin to stab him to death, although Orin does so inadvertently. According to Orin, Childress, a small man, always had a big mouth and the bad habit of playing around with his knife. On the day that Orin killed Childress, Childress, who was drunk, preceded a knife attack by demanding an insignificant amount of money that he said Orin owed him. Friendships between black men seem always to be tenuous because of the poverty and degradation that afflict the black community. The pressures on Childress were overwhelming the day he stepped over the edge, trying to hurt his friend, and fell to his own death. After Orin has been imprisoned, there are pitiful jail scenes in which blacks talk to those incarcerated through the cold, impersonal bars. Blacks are caged and separated from each other, their lives fragmented and unhealthy. The situation of Orin, Bernice, Childress, and other blacks is a bad one.

A jail scene between Orin and Bernice constitutes the next to last section of part 3. A short section at the book's end focuses on Anthony, a young hospital attendant whom Littleman has tried to indoctrinate, and reinforces the idea that black experience involves self-destructive powerlessness. Anthony is a failure in school, a student whose motivation is low largely as a result of his black environment. Littleman tries to teach him to think for himself and not to fear whites and white power, but the strength of racism makes Anthony fear the nurse who is his superior. He seems downtrodden; he does not relate well to the lessons that Littleman tries to teach.

In the basement of the hospital, two older black dishwashers tease and taunt Anthony about his naivete and sexual inexperience. He is highly irritated by them but feels helpless when he tries to produce the repartee that would stop their insults. These men have a kind of status superior to Anthony's because they are full-time workers older than he. It makes their day to prove that they are superior to him. As much as Anthony resents the men, one can imagine that one day he will achieve their status as a full-time menial worker and will tease and taunt other young, black part-time workers. He will not rise beyond the submissive role of hospital attendant.

The account of Anthony in part 3 affords further evidence of black frustration and impotence. It punctuates the statement made by Orin and his family and friends that the depth of the oppressive black reality is partly responsible for killing the plan conceived to change it. In the last paragraph of *Lynchers,* as Anthony, his inarticulate frustration intensified by Littleman's death, knocks over the contents of a nurses's station, it is clear that for black people the legacy of the "Matter Prefatory" remains powerful.

In spite of Wideman's belief that the black community is impotent and bent on self-destruction, he portrays black feeling and experience in a graphic and memorable way. The world that he creates is less dominated by white literary vision than that in *A Glance Away,* and he focuses on life in the black community much more here than in *Hurry Home.* Many people can identify with parts of the conspirators' imaginative vision, if not with the plan itself, and the conspirators' intent to effect mass black action and militant revolution fits with the intentions and practices of black Americans even before Nat Turner. But not only does *Lynchers* indicate how the advanced militant guard of black people thinks; it portrays black people generally as so beaten down that they think only about subsisting, often living lives little removed in quality from those of the blacks in the "Matter Prefatory." There is much black longing, pain, suffering, and struggle for liberation in *Lynchers.*

According to my analysis, *Lynchers* shows that intellectuals and thinking, introspective black men will lose themselves in contemplation of the paradoxes and pitiful conditions of the black community, or the powerless, oppressed position of the community will, to a significant extent at least, doom them to ludicrous, ineffectual positions of imaginative ingenuity, where they will not affect the community at all. These characters are not the traditional thinking intellectuals such as Cecil in *Home* or Wideman himself early in his career, but they are very imaginative, creative people whom Wideman distinguishes from the majority of blacks. In Wideman's views, the black community desperately needs change and improvement, and these intellectuals could play a part in bringing it about. Viewed from this perspective, the outlook for intellectuals and for thinking blacks who want to be activists, as well as for the black community, is bleak.

The other characters in the community reflect the oppressive conditions about which Wideman speaks and lack any perspective, even on themselves; they certainly cannot solve their problem. These characters are self-destructive, mean, cruel, simpleminded, or uninventive. They should not be a part of change or work to precipitate it in the black community.

Lynchers carries Wideman to the point in his career where, as a writer and intellectual, he can fully develop the black voice that is first evident in *Lynchers*. Wideman remains enmeshed in the problems he associates with the concerned black intellectual for some time after *Lynchers*—for eight years, in fact, until he writes his next book of fiction. But *Lynchers* allows Wideman to soften the pessimistic modernist voice that he uses to describe the black community so that he can start to articulate the rich, indigenous cultural framework of the community in a black voice. *Lynchers* moves Wideman to a point where he will be able to talk about and examine the aspects of black culture that are enriching, nurturing, and sustaining for black people.

By making a black worldview central and setting the book in the external world of the black community, Wideman has been able to move beyond a derivative white perspective and a specifically derivative style and form to start developing a strong black voice. Wideman's style and form in *Lynchers* are more uniquely black than they are in either of his first two books. Wideman has incorporated a very general legacy from other twentieth-century modernist writers into a black worldview. In *Lynchers*, the modernist voice is no longer the only strong voice.

Wideman's use of surrealism in Littleman's description of the black god's birth shows how he borrows generally from the techniques of modernism while at the same time emphasizing black elements.

> The gods of fire, of wine, of blood are not coincidental. They are the faint impressions of mortal men blown up a million times. History is a

consuming, crackling fire and time is a vast bland screen and all that men can understand or believe is the play of shadows, the outlines of men or nations caught for an instant before they drop into the flame and ascend in the shapeless smoke endlessly climbing the screen. Most men read the smoke, most men pass so easily to oblivion they are smoke. But some are free. Are gods because they print themselves against the screen. Then the smoke readers, the smoke itself cannot ignore them, will never quite be the same again.

To free the Black God I will drop the hanged cop into the fire. The contorted silhouette will flash darkly on the screen. There will be no turning back, no hiding in the shivering smoke. The lynched white cop will not only be an ineradicable element in the future, but it will seem as if he and his lynchers have always existed, patiently waiting to be perceived, a mystery to be worshipped.

To tear such a hole in history. To assist at the birth of a God. These are worth my sacrifice. I would lie here a millennium, if my organs continue to function, calm as a sail waiting for wind. [172–73]

The vision expressed through the broadly surrealistic modernist form is specifically very charcteristic of black nationalistic thinking and is part of the beginning of Wideman's development of a black voice. The passage takes us from the unfamiliar surrealistic conception of historical reality and most men's anonymous places in that reality, to the description of Littleman symbolically making an imprint for black people in historical reality in the second paragraph, to Littleman's patient waiting for the fruition of his dream in the third paragraph. What is unique here is the black nationalistic worldview. Littleman has convinced the other three conspirators that they can achieve the ultimate militant, nationalistic revolution by the abstract and symbolic, but magical, act of lynching a white cop. They can change the whole direction of history in this way.

Some general observations about the strengths of *Lynchers'* portrayals seem in order. Littleman is the ideologue whose plan may appear to be total illusion in the eyes of most readers. But what is so striking about Littleman is not the practicality of his plan but the justice, the rightness of his thinking. Many observers would agree with Littleman, just as they would with black nationalistic figures in Afro-American history, that blacks must control their lives and that blacks must positively reverse the direction of Afro-American history. Littleman's belief in violence as a means to bring about this reversal makes him an authentic militant black nationalist; whether or not many observers would agree to using violent means to attain justice is of course another matter.

Thomas's dilemma of being trapped between the need to combat racism, on one side, and his preference for compassion, on the other side, is very recognizably a black predicament. Positions of higher status and class, even in relation only to other blacks, have made many individuals falter in the pursuit of justice, whether or not violence was considered a means to the desired end. And then there is the question of violence and killing. Who can perpetrate violence without initially having a well-formed, popularly supported organization behind him? Perhaps very few individuals as humane and compassionate as Thomas can do so. And the question of whether Thomas has the moral right to hurt and kill for justice and freedom has been a heavy one in the black community, as the tension between nationalistic groups and groups concerned with black civil rights well shows.

Saunders is frightening but very believable and recognizable. He is someone who has faced too much poverty, pain, and suffering. Saunders's upbringing in the ghetto has made him cold and callous; if he were not, he would probably be insane or seriously incapacitated. Yes, Saunders can kill. But he is no different from countless other blacks who kill and do violence because of the way in which their environment has molded them.

Orin and Bernice present responses to racism and poverty in the ghetto that are both accurate and memorable. We have no way of knowing what kind of relationship Orin and Bernice would have if they were living a comfortable, middle-class existence, but poverty and racism have clearly worsened the quality of their lives. In part Orin needs to be constantly in the streets partying and chasing women (he is called Sweetman) in order to compensate for his lack of power and of a sense of self-worth, problems that are his because he is black and poor. He feels in many ways inadequate to take care of his family, so he proves his adequacy by entertaining and pleasing women on a short-term basis. Bernice finds that she must sit at home in impoverished surroundings while Orin is away for long periods. Being a poor black woman, she finds herself locked in her predicament. In all likelihood she could not escape the ghetto even if she left Orin. So she resigns herself to a life of misery, while Orin resigns himself to a lifetime of frustration.

Lynchers fails to describe the experience of blacks who attain success and fulfillment and thus does not achieve a full black voice. Still, the painful, frustrating experience that it portrays is one side of black American history and its presentation here constitutes a step toward the development of a black voice. Overall, *Lynchers* describes black frustration with the black condition very well.

In *Lynchers* Wideman is as faithful to the rhythm of black language as he is in the Homewood trilogy. Furthermore, in *Lynchers* language carries tension and suspense. We sense that the lives of characters hang in the balance and that the destiny of all black people is at stake. This tension is lacking in the later works, with the possible exception of *Brothers*. The language successfully conveys the black experience of frustration, struggle, and ultimate calamity.

Hiding Place

Writers, Community, and Voice

After writing his first three books, Wideman decided that he wanted
to reach a larger black audience and to accomplish some new things
in his fiction (Samuels 1983:43), in essence to penetrate more deeply
into the black experience and to examine it from a more positive
black perspective. To achieve this end, Wideman immersed himself
in other black writers and also tried to learn by listening to what
people in his own family said (Samuels 1983:44–45, 52–53). As a
result Wideman learned about the many substantive and indigenous
aspects of the black community; the black community was by no
means hopeless, as he depicted it in *The Lynchers*. The mainstream
modernist pessimism that dominated *A Glance Away*, *Hurry Home*,
and *Lynchers* was not appropriate and adequate to encompass the
possibilities and resources of black culture. Black culture was not
locked in pessimism; it had its own devices to deal with its

problems. Wideman had to find ways to capture black cultural richness and resourcefulness in his writing.

In *Hiding Place* (1981), Wideman finally brings together what he learns from other black writers and from personal family experiences to achieve the black voice that subsumes mainstream modernism and articulates black cultural tradition-myth, language, rituals, and folkways. In *Hiding Place*, however, the black intellectual is conspicuously in the background. Wideman has learned from other black writers that the mainstream modernist idea of the separation between intellectual-artist and community does not necessarily hold true. Before he integrates the black intellectual into the community, however, he uses the narrative in *Hiding Place* to show that the folk characters can transcend their alienation, anger, despair, and pessimism to find the resources in black culture that will allow them to live meaningful lives as a part of the black family and the community. In *Hiding Place* Wideman fictionally discovers for himself the black resources that indicate the presence of a substantive culture. In *Damballah*, he integrates the black intellectual into the black community; this book was also published in 1981. *Hiding Place* begins the second stage of Wideman's career, the Homewood trilogy stage.

Several critical essays about black writing, most of them published during the eight-year hiatus between *Lynchers* and *Hiding Place*, indicate what Wideman learned from other black writers about black cultural resources and about speaking in a black voice. Ernest Gaines, with his clear, straightforward style, as a writer seems to have little in common with Wideman, but Wideman's essay "*Of Love and Dust*: A Reconsideration" shows that Gaines exerted a profound impact on Wideman.

The following discussion shows how Gaines's conception of myth and tradition counters, for example, T. S. Eliot's mainstream modernist view that myth and tradition had become stagnant and empty. To describe Gaines's creation in *Of Love and Dust* Wideman uses the key term "mythic archetype" (76). The term refers to Gaines's creation of a story that depicts black characters in an oppressive world of the present where they can draw on the traditions, values, and customs of the black past, "the best that has been thought and said by generations of Afro-Americans in the crucible of the South" (77). It is also important that Wideman speaks of Gaines's concept of time in *Dust* as not being "straight line clock time" moving "from *once upon to the end*. Time is a medium in which the characters

float, a river where no one can step into the same place twice" (79).
The characters may not exactly be able to repeat the past, but they
are always immersed in a flow and swirl of black traditions. They
are constantly being sustained, enriched, and renewed by these
traditions. Black culture carries within itself the seeds of its own
continuation and revitalization. Jim Kelly, the main character and
the primary repository and carrier of black culture, continues to
disseminate and remake that culture.

Wideman's comments about *Dust*'s sustaining, enriching tradition
are important because in large part they are applicable to the
Homewood trilogy, to *Hiding Place* and *Damballah*, both published
in 1981, and to *Sent for You Yesterday* (1983). In these three books,
the stories incorporate a level of black "mythic archetype" that
informs and is informed by the present. Specifically, in *Hiding Place*,
the setting is very much the present, and the book deals with the
problems of frustration and alienation in the present. But the
positive changes in the story grow out of the mythic traditions,
values, and customs of an archetypal black folk community. That is,
the values, traditions, and customs that save Bess and Tommy are
embedded in a folk community with roots that lie ultimately in the
concepts of extended family and community in various African
cultures. (*Damballah*, which through its first story shows the clear
link between African and black American communities, makes the
point even more clearly than *Hiding Place*.) These values, traditions,
and customs are almost timeless, and it is up to Bess and Tommy to
mine them and reassert their place in the community. I will discuss
this subject at greater length in connection with *Hiding Place*.

From black writer Albert Murray, Wideman learned important
things about the use of black language that he needed to know to
attain a black voice; in Wideman's essay "*Stomping the Blues*:
Ritual in Black Music and Speech," he discusses Murray's emphasis
on the "ritualistic qualities of Black speech" and the "magical,
evocative, transforming qualities of Black expressive culture" (44).
According to Wideman, Murray analyzes these concepts and incorporates them into the structure of *Stomping the Blues*. Wideman's
black language is ritualistic, magical, and transformative in *Hiding
Place*, *Damballah*, and *Yesterday*. If we focus again on *Hiding Place*,
we can see specific examples of the way in which black language is
rhetorical, ritualistic, designed to affect reality by its repetitive,
incantatory qualities. Bess is transformed to a significant extent
because she repeats over and over to herself, and to Tommy, impor-

tant events of the past, family connections, and key words and phrases that link her and Tommy to the past and magically make him materialize for her as a relative; she does not accept him as a relative during the first section of the book. The ritualization of language has much to do with its nonlinear function as evoker of the timeless qualities and values of the black community. Again, I will return to this subject.

Wideman discusses black writers' use of the ritualistic, allusive qualities of language in two other essays, "Defining the Black Voice in Fiction" and "Charles Chesnutt and the WPA Narratives: The Oral and Literate Roots of Afro-American Literature" (in Gates and Davis 1985). In "Black Voice," Wideman contrasts language usage in the works of Phillis Wheatley and Gayl Jones, and implies that Jones exerts a general influence, if not a direct one. During Wheatley's time, when black oral expression carried heavy, clear connotations of inferiority, black oral expression in print carried this same inferior connotation. It noted the trivial, the superficial, and the ignorant. Black oral expression "lost its depth in time, the link with the ancestors and sources of vitality. . . , its allusiveness, the sources of moral and legal authority" (Gates and Davis 1985:79). Jones was one of the recent black writers responsible for making black language primary, for establishing its authority and important ritualistic role in connecting black people on the mythic, archetypal level of community. In the writing of Jones and other black writers since Wheatley, language carries the mythic, timeless qualities of the black community that link it to the wisdom of the ancestors, that allow language in the present to be allusive and tie the contemporary into the eternal, ideal qualities of blackness.

Charles Chesnutt, who wrote at the turn of the twentieth century, struggled significantly to establish the authenticity of black speech and to exploit its richness at a time when it carried the code of inferiority. Cunningly and cleverly, Chesnutt in his conjure stories made black speech the main frame of reference and used such black speech rituals as signifying and such techniques as repetition to manipulate his audience (Gates and Davis 1985:66–67, 77). These rituals and techniques heavily inform Wideman's own recent writing.

Wideman's immersion in other black writers also profoundly affected his ability to use black speech and black tradition to achieve a dominant black voice. These black writers whom Wideman mentions having read in the essays include: Imamu Baraka,

Richard Wright, Ralph Ellison, James Baldwin, James Weldon Johnson, Zora Neale Hurston, and Paul Laurence Dunbar. Wideman read voraciously (Samuels 1983:44–45), and he probably read a number of other writers as well.

As preparation for his focus on the positive, sustaining qualities of the folk community in *Hiding Place*, Wideman distanced his intellectual perspective, which had been shaped by white, modernist writers and by a tradition that ignored black culture or treated it as inferior. He did so by directing his creative imagination to the level of black folk tradition, wisdom, and struggle in the community. Wideman adapts his imagination to folk voices, and the story emerges from the folk perspective, projecting problems from a folk viewpoint, showing the folk using their cultural wisdom to deal with their problems. There emerges perspective outside the conscious understanding of the folk characters; it stresses the richness of the folk language and cultural traditions and the inextricable ties of traditions in the present to the past and future. This perspective certainly invites intellectual analysis. This perspective emerges, however, through the thoughts and actions of the people; an intellectual narrator or intellectual character does not impose it from an alien standpoint. Since Wideman adapts his voice and viewpoint to that of the folk characters who actively and effectively cope in their world, we do not encounter well-intentioned, intellectual black characters who become trapped in their own imaginations and rendered ineffectual by the level of their thinking, as is the case in *Lynchers*. Wideman's approach deepens and enriches our appreciation of black folk wisdom, although the folk characters do not become fully aware of the broad implications and effects of their practices and beliefs.

Perhaps the most direct connection between *Hiding Place* and Wideman's essays is evident in his discussions of Ernest Gaines and Albert Murray. As we see from the lives of Clement, Bess, and Tommy, *Hiding Place* shows daily life as involving alienation, frustration, and pain in the present. Without denying the fact of this existence, the overarching world of black mythic archetype allows the characters to tap into positive values. While living the pain, fear, and isolation of the present, the characters securely move into the future by drawing upon the events, traditions, values, and customs of their familial, communal, and racial past. They use the "best" that has been thought, done, and experienced by past generations of blacks in Homewood, in the American South, and finally in Africa.

As previously noted, the southern and African connection clearly emerges in the first story in *Damballah*, which Wideman wants to be read in conjunction with *Hiding Place* (Samuels 1983:45–46).

Wideman continues to stress the inner life in *Hiding Place*, as he does in *Home* and *Lynchers*, but the internal is no longer a place of imaginative isolation. It has become a place where the characters address their problems with voices steeped in black culture. The black folk voices often speak internally but from a psychic region where the characters partake of the saving world of mythic archetype and use what they find to affect their actions in the present. The characters draw on the repository of memory to find the positive, timeless values and traditions of black community and ancestry. *Hiding Place* is full of dreams, and dreams to some extent come from this same region of mind and memory. In contrast to the heavily mainstream modernist thematic and formal structure of *Lynchers*, dreams are not just nightmarish visions but are sometimes supernatural perceptions that lead characters to meaningful insights. Memory centered in the mythic, archetypal world is also at least partly responsible for dictating the characters' language, and the ritualization of language reinvokes the traditional values in the present. In this sense, language is magic in a different, more positive and substantive way than it has been in *Home* and *Lynchers*. Dreams and language contribute to Wideman's black voice in *Hiding Place*.

Despite the ability of the characters to tap into traditional values and ideals of the ancestral past, Wideman does not romanticize their lives and show them as being able to solve their problems in simple, easy ways. The problems of daily existence truly challenge the characters, and their memories, dreams, and language use do not infallibly guide them and center them in traditional ideals. Bess's memory is choked with bitterness, and her dreams are often laced with nightmarish qualities. Tommy is always reaching for the perfect and ideal in his dreams but often finds himself with the nightmarish, as does Bess. And Tommy has been a successful singer and rapper. During the crises of his life, however, his talk produces very few desired results and certainly no magic transformations. Nevertheless, through a painful process very much affected by the flaws of human nature and the detrimental conditions of daily life, the characters do use their memories, dreams, and language rituals to gain access to the world of black traditional values. At the end, these values produce a positive relationship between Bess and

Tommy, give each of them a positive sense of self, and reintegrate Bess into family and community.

Clement is a young man who runs errands for Bess and for the community. He is a folk character who is a vehicle for black tradition and also a pervasive connecting spirit in the community. His apparent retardation makes people take him for granted, so that he is often ignored. Clement moves through the community carrying many of its positive attitudes, habits, and traditional values. In many ways, Clement symbolizes the traditions that pervade the community although the community is unaware of them. His seeming feeblemindedness makes him a good conduit for the traditions that shape the community daily but lie hidden and unnoticed beneath its surface.

Clement lives at one of the prime community centres, in Big Bob's barbershop. The barbershop is his shelter and resting place, his home, and the people who enter the barbershop are his family and his social outlet. He cleans the barbershop and thereby takes care of his home and community. Clement's strong family feelings go further, however. In spite of the fact that he is an orphan and does not know his mother, he develops a very positive image of her and guards it, unarticulated, in his mind.

Clement's actions also unite alienated segments of the community. He is the line of communication between Big Bob and Miss Claudine, seemingly hostile opposites representing the profane and ungodly and the conservative and refined, respectively. He keeps Bess in contact with others in the community who try to avoid her totally because they fear her strange powers. He takes the number Bess is playing to Big Bob, who is shaking and trembling with fear, and carries Bess's money back to her from Big Bob. When Clement sees John, Tommy's educated brother and clearly Wideman's surrogate, who lives in Wyoming and feels an easiness with Tommy, sometimes almost hating him (102), he recognizes, as John cannot, that John and Tommy have underlying similarities and share a certain power. He sees in John the same "eyes of the ghost [Tommy] on Bruston Hill. Eyes that could scream across a room, through a wall" (104). Clement's acceptance of the relationship that binds him, Bess, and Tommy indicates the legitimacy of Bess and Tommy's connection and further reinforces family and community ties. Finally, Clement is in touch with the essence of communication and connection in the community. Just as he recognizes the power in John and Tommy's eyes to "scream across a room, through a wall," he also feels Bess's ability to look through walls (34). Throughout the book, he hears and responds to Bess's "silent call."

In section 1 of *Hiding Place*, Bess alienates herself atop Bruston Hill, occupying her mind with cynical, bitter thoughts, reminding herself several times that she has disavowed Christianity and is ready to die. Her dominant thoughts concern the tragic, senseless death of her only son, born late after years of agonizing about her failure to have a child, and her times with her husband, also long dead and in the past.

Early in the book, a story of spring and her youth tries to force itself into Bess's consciousness.

> But she was young again and it was spring and she'd listen till whoever was telling the story got tired of telling it.
>
> Her fingers played in the coarse grass [in Westinghouse Park in Homewood]. Over her shoulder and to the left toward the train tracks and the foot bridge, she could hear the chains of swings creaking. Somebody would be flying, gulping the blue air and trying to swallow it, keep it down before the next rush, the next mouthful when the swing soared to the end of its tether and you thought it just might pitch you into the middle of the steel rails.
>
> Bess . . . Bess.
>
> It was her man [her husband] calling. But he was long dead. He couldn't be telling the story. No one was telling the story because the sky was falling and the music dying and her man's voice was far away now, far and high away as the birds. Her man was a speck. A raisin, a seed, then a tiny hole in the sky like a stone makes just for a second when it hits the water.
>
> Bess . . . Bess.
>
> She is saying her own name alone in the light that is not morning yet or night still but in between somewhere so she's not sure either has happened or will happen again. *Bess.* Saying her name so it's like *the end* and chases the story away. [24]

This episode takes place in the time between dawn and night, and the potentially resurrecting story of youth and spring comes to Bess from the recesses of memory and dream. In this case, memory and dream would draw Bess back into life, but the rhythmless repetition of Bess's name cuts the story off, at best hints at an abortive call-and-response ritual. There is, at this point in *Hiding Place*, no language–ritual process to make the essence of the story real.

Long after this early episode, Bess remains trapped in the realm of negative memories, bad dreams, and nasty, cynical talk, but as she interacts more and more with Tommy, her memory brings to

consciousness the family stories and community history and traditions that will make her a loving, caring person again and will
enable her to reenter the community. Bess keeps remembering the
times when Homewood was better and she was a part of a sharing,
supportive, religious community there. An important aspect of the
secular side of that community was the blues music of her husband,
Bill Campbell, and John French, Tommy's grandfather. This music
also carried a communal spirit, particularly in the way that it tied
life in Homewood with life in the American southern past (49–50).
Bess was a part of a large, active family when she was a child, and
the togetherness of the family always made the good overshadow the
bad. She remembers, too, when she was older and bitter and family
members tried, ironically, to draw sustenance from her evil power by
having her kiss their babies. Bess remembers especially the time
when Tommy's sister Shirley brought her baby to be saved after the
doctors had given up hope. Shirley's baby died, and Bess went to the
funeral. The memory of the baby's funeral and a sad-looking Tommy
at the funeral, with "grave dust all over his shoes" (54), starts Bess on
her way back into family and community.

> The boy sleeping in her shed was a Lawson and his sister was Shirley,
> Lizabeth's middle child. She had seen the boy at the funeral when they
> buried Shirley's baby.
>   She said the words again to herself *buried Shirley's baby* and the words
> were what she had been avoiding all along since she saw the boy's face.
> But she couldn't help herself. Even if the words rocked the flimsy shack,
> rocked her soul as it plummeted with the crashing walls down toward the
> center of the earth. Sooner or later she'd put the faces together and say
> something like *buried Shirley's baby* and saying the words would be like
> hearing her man whistling the blues knowing her first step toward him
> would crack the earth knowing the crack was too high to get over and too
> wide to get around and too low to get under but knowing she can't help
> herself and moving toward that sound, toward the emptiness which is all
> there is which is what she knows she will find after she has stepped
> toward him and the earth has swallowed him again, swallowed his hair
> brushing blues and all there is of him left to love. Those words she said to
> herself, couldn't help saying to herself *buried Shirley's baby* moved her
> off of Bruston Hill and down again into the Homewood streets where
> people were singing and crying and making love and losing children and
> changing names like names could make a difference, like any of it made a
> difference. [50–51]

The tragic words of recent family history, reinforced by their
repetition, carry a density, weight, and power that evoke family

associations and draw Bess into the rhythm, flow, and swirl—the "singing and crying and making love and losing children and changing names"—of the Homewood streets, where people are doing many of the things they have done for generations. The words also remind Bess of the emptiness she associates with the loss of her husband, but within this painful feeling, there is the full, all-encompassing support of God on the part of the individual and the community that is incorporated into the traditional Negro spiritual sung over the generations. Somewhere in the tragic words, hidden under the terrible loss of her husband, is awareness of a God who is "too high to get over and too wide to get around and too low to get under." The presence of this God may be somewhat threatening, but black tradition stresses much more that this God is a protector of individual, family, and community.

Funerals are important experiences because they bring family and community together, and the absence of the dead person forces those gathered to be more conscious of family and community. Especially for Bess, since the dead person is a child, the near-ritual repetition of the words that capture the experience—"buried Shirley's baby"—forces her to make family connections and eventually to return to community life and traditions. After her repetition of the words, she "couldn't stop making the connections she knew she'd have to make" (51).

Language ritualization is part of the process that makes Tommy real for Bess and makes her connection to him real, right, necessary, ineluctable. Its role is very clear in a fairly long passage at the beginning of section 2.

Don't you think I knew you was out there. Don't you think I saw those long feet sticking out my shed. How you gon hide those long feet, those long legs. I knew you was out there. Where else you gon be?

She said it to herself a dozen times before she said it to him. And didn't say it to him when she shook him awake. No, she was quiet then, quiet as the morning which wasn't even morning yet, quiet as dawn, as the dew and darkness still hanging on when she wrapped her sweater around the nightgown and pulled on her coat over both and shuffled outside in her slippers to shake him awake. She was as quiet as the half sleep world when she took hold to the stick leaning against her bed and dragged it and dragged herself out to the shed where she knew he'd be sleeping. That quiet when she grabbed his shoulders like she grabbed the stick laid beside her bed in case him or some other nigger was crazy enough to try and take her house, grabbed the knob of bone in his shoulder which felt

like the knob of her walking stick and shook him awake without saying
what she'd said a dozen times to herself beginning when she dreamed the
feet and again when she looked through the walls, through the black
night and saw them poking out her shed and again when she made herself
awake, made herself struggle with the sweater and pull on the coat saying
it a dozen times at least before she crossed to the shed and shook him
awake. And didn't say it out loud till he was sitting at the table again like
something the cat drug in and she was starting a fire in the stove because
he sat there shivering, his eyes closed, a shadow hardly more real than the
shapes moving on the ceiling as the stove flared to life and she got the
kettle and got that water going.

Then she spoke to the shadow as if speaking to it might stop its
shivering, make it real.

Don't you think I knew you was out there. Don't you think I saw those
long feet sticking out my shed? How you gon hide those long feet, those
long legs. I knew you was out there. Where else you gon be? [91–92]

Bess's words to herself in the traditional Homewood vernacular
appear first, and repetition in these lines ties succeeding lines
together and links separated lines in a way which suggests the
regularity of ritual practice. The third-person narrator then takes
over and reiterates several times that Bess repeated the words to
"herself a dozen times . . . and didn't say it to him. . . . [She] shook
him awake without saying what she'd said a dozen times to herself
. . . and didn't say it aloud until he was sitting at the table." And
throughout this section, the narrator's repetitious description of
Bess's ritual accentuates her repetition and ritualization of language.
After Bess goes through the ritual repetition of words to herself
several times, she finally vocalizes the ritual to Tommy, the
"shadow," as if she were making him "real." (Bess repeats the words
again later in the book.)

Tommy is indeed "real" for Bess now; her whole attitude toward
him has changed. She wants to shelter, nourish, and protect her
relative. The language ritual that she undergoes makes the supportive relationship true and certain once and for all. Certainly, Tommy
is where Bess says he is, but as previously noted, the repetition of
the words gives his place there positive meaning and significance—
an inevitability, necessity, and rightness. The vernacular is not the
only thing here with a long black tradition. The use of this kind of
language ritual process to achieve desired, sometimes tangible,
results is traditional in the black community in religious services
and in such secular language practices as signifying.

Characters' dreams in *Hiding Place* are often horrible or nightmarish, but dreams can help tap the characters' repository of traditional values. In addition to Bess's word ritual, the preceding passage incorporates a physical ritual, a ritual of actions; as part of the process of making Tommy's relationship to her positive and meaningful, Bess must go out to the shed to touch him physically, shake him awake, and bring him inside. To carry out these actions she must dream about him in the shed: "she dreamed the feet and . . . looked through the walls, through the black night and saw them poking out her shed." The physical ritual consequently depends upon her knowledge of Tommy's place close to her, which is buried deep in her mind; the dream brings it out. Positive values of family connection may be so deeply buried that they must surface in dreams, but the values and traditions are there. The characters draw on them; they affect the present.

Another example of Bess's magical use of language to achieve concrete results is her ritualization of the numbers 753, which she plays and wins.

> . . . seven five three floating before my eyes like those smoky white letters . . . in the sky. . . . seven days and seven sins and seven come eleven if you shooting crap. And five got that hook. Five is a fisher. Five is fever. Five is staying alive. . . . Seven-five-three. That's the middle, that's the heart of the odds. Three right next to the gate but it got to wait. Can't get over. Can't get under. Can't get around. But three's trying. Circling everywhich way. Got curves and straight and zigzags. Got a hook too like five. But three is at the gate. Three is two faces and two eyes can't see each other but sees everything else. Three got a mirror in its belly. But how you [Clement] gon know what I'm talking about. . . . I'm just playing numberology and trickology. Ain't nothing to it anyway. Just got lucky with 753. [142]

In this passage, the language ritual evokes no positive traditional values in the present, but it is both traditionally and currently a part of the black survival mechanism (a way of getting money and putting food on the table). Bess says at first that the number "just come to me is all," saw it "plain as day" (140) and later says that she "just got lucky." But in fact her ability to ritualize the numbers—to ritualize the words "seven," "five," "three"—has much to do with her win.

A large part of Tommy's problem is that he has almost lost touch with tradition. Tommy, who is the same character as Robby in *Brothers and Keepers*, is a part of the 1960s generation. The 1960s were a time of significant disruption in the Homewood community, when the place was physically devastated and black youngsters turned to drugs and vicious crimes. During these years the flow of tradition between generations slowed. As a consequence, it is much more difficult for Tommy to use his memory to tie into positive values and traditions. Also, his dreams are most often nightmarish and unproductive and his language empty and substanceless. It is hard for him to ritualize his language for positive results. He does show signs of centering himself in black tradition by the end, though.

In Wideman's essay on *Of Love and Dust,* he remarks that time in the book is not "a straight line from *once upon to the end*" (79); instead, time and tradition flow in a circle, and the characters exist in the flow. Thus a tradition perpetuates itself, and linear movement means loss of the positive effects of tradition's movement. In the following passage from *Hiding Place,* Tommy shows that he is outside tradition, trapped in linear time, and cannot use his language to create the positive effects he wants to create, the positive effects that Bess creates so well through language rituals.

> Once upon a time. Once upon a time, he thought, if them stories I been hearing all my life are true, once upon a time they said God's green earth was peaceful and quiet. Seems like people bigger then. They had time to listen, time to talk and room to move around in. Aunt Aida talking about people like they giants. That world was bigger, slower and he'd get jumpy, get lost in it. . . . But once upon a time him and [his wife] Sarah alone in the middle of the night. Just the two of them and the world sleeping and you get mixed up. Can't tell whose stomach growls, who moans, whose warm juice running down your thigh. Because it's late and the city's asleep outside the window, outside the walls. You're in a story. There's room enough to do what you need to do, what you have to do. . . .
>
> The stillness unbroken. Sarah rolls closer to him and rises slightly on her elbow so the ring of darker brown around her nipples is visible an instant as the covers fall away from her brown shoulders and he swallows hard because those soft eyes on her chest have a way of seeing through him and around him and taking his breath away. . . . He swallows hard in the stillness because he is seeing another life, a life long gone. Then he is nothing. Smaller than nothing and alone. Stories are lies and Mother Bess pigging down her soup brings him back. Her loud slurping on the soup drowns the noise of his blood, the noise of his heart. [79–80]

Tommy's attempt to tell the story shows figuratively how he is outside the positive, supportive flow of black tradition. Tommy's story moves from "once upon a time" to a finality, to "a life long gone." Past this point, he is "nothing and alone," with no other individual or community to help or support him. There is no traditional repository of saving stories invested with positive values and belief, with examples of family and community love and togetherness. Tommy's ritual of storytelling produces "nothing."

Bess does establish a truly caring and nurturing relationship with Tommy, however, and this relationship with Bess allows Tommy to start the process of finding the traditional patterns and reaching out to others in family and community. The passage below shows Tommy beginning to draw on black tradition for strength and support.

> He says, *Well, that's that, old woman,* not knowing exactly what he means, saying the words because he's heard them before and said them before so they come easy but he doesn't know what he means, hadn't planned to say anything until the words come out just as he said them, almost as if they had found him and didn't bother to let him know what they were talking about. *Well, that's that.* And he addressed the words to her because she was in the dark room with him, because she had taught him to plant [a garden], because she sent the boy [Clement] for Iron City, because she was sipping nasty shine in nasty water with him and it had been three days now and he was tired now, and high enough now to need somebody else to speak to, to draw him out of the fog into which he was sinking. The fog of his own thoughts, his own body, his own life which was settling over him again like the darkness draping her shack. [147]

Tommy is coming out of himself and is ritualizing words that will enable him to connect with Bess, who is friend, protector, teacher, and mother, true to her ironic nickname, Mother Bess. Tommy's words are ones that he has heard before and has said before, but they speak themselves, as if they were using him. He is falling into a pattern and is ritualizing the words in that pattern. The words are making real the traditional relationships of his family and community.

Shortly after Tommy says these words, he puts his life, with its fear and uncertainty, and Homewood, with all its recent hard times, in perspective. He understands that racism has been responsible for taking away many of the chances for the recent generation in Homewood. But still, he is going back into the Homewood streets to face life, including the consequences of the murder with which he is charged, and will "do the best I can cause I ain't scared" (151). By the end, Tommy sounds very much like the tough, resilient character in the black blues tradition as practiced in the black community and as presented by such black writers as Ralph Ellison and Albert Murray.

Hiding Place maintains a realistic focus on the problems of contemporary black Homewood while at the same time showing how the characters use an ideal store of traditional folkways to enrich their lives and maintain themselves for the future. The characters, including Tommy, float in the stream of black tradition, and they will consequently always be more or less in contact with the values and beliefs that will save and resurrect them. In their relationship near the end, Bess and Tommy dredge the depths of tradition quite thoroughly. Their present situation is obviously not ideal, but it is informed by a tradition of ideals developed over the generations and still being augmented by the present generations. Wideman attains his black voice in *Hiding Place* by portraying the alienation, frustration, pain, and pessimism common to mainstream modernism and black culture, problems brought into focus by the mainstream modernist perspective adopted in previous books, through the medium of supportive black cultural traditions.

Wideman makes John, Tommy's educated brother, a very minor character who is out of touch with the Homewood community. Uncle Carl thinks John lives in Colorado, but John actually lives in Wyoming, where "it's a good place to raise children" (101). In the Brass Rail bar, where John has a conversation with Uncle Carl, he looks odd and talks formally, prompting the bar woman, Violet, to say that he is shy but educated and "could talk that talk if he wanted to" (103). Violet is being kind, but she sees that John is from a different world, one out of touch with Homewood. In the overall context of the book, when John says that he comes close to hating Tommy at times, he certainly shows his lack of understanding. He is out of contact with the community and understands nothing about the toughness of the struggle that Tommy's generation has had to face. Tommy has slipped outside the main circulatory channels of the black tradition, but John is even further outside the flow.

As I said at the beginning of this chapter, Wideman has learned from other black writers that the intellectual need not be outside the community as many mainstream modernist writers have portrayed him. Although John is outside in this instance, *Hiding Place* makes it clear that he does not have to be. Clement, a focal point for the tradition and the community in the novel, perceives that John is very much like his brother Tommy, who is a product of the community and is reestablishing his ties. Wideman has now fictionally evolved a black voice to articulate the rich, substantive black cultural tradition. In *Damballah*, he can now integrate the black intellectual into the strong black cultural tradition that will accept him if he is capable of accepting it.

The strong achievements of the first three books (especially *Lynchers*) notwithstanding, Wideman reaches his highest achievement in *Hiding Place* through his articulation of the book's milieu in a dominant black voice. The crucial thing for Wideman was the time he spent relearning the intimate details of his family and community and absorbing the black tradition as other black writers present it. Wideman is impressive in his overall rendition of black cultural tradition. His portrayal of black language, rituals, myth, and folkways is skillful, accurate, and effective. With *Hiding Place*, Wideman clearly forges his place among twentieth-century black writers who have made mainstream literary modernism a part of their dominant black literary voice.

Damballah

The Intellectual and the Folk Voice

In *Damballah* (1981), the second book of the Homewood trilogy, Wideman presents a wide range of black folk characters who draw on various aspects of the black cultural tradition—including stories, folk beliefs and rituals, religious songs, and religious rituals—to triumph over racism, poverty, hardship, and pain. Wideman now brings a black voice to themes that received a mainstream modernist treatment in the early books. Wideman speaks in a black voice even louder and deeper than his black voice in *Hiding Place* because the range of characters and folk forms, rituals, and beliefs is broader. Here, in contrast to *Hiding Place*, the emphasis from the first part of the book is on ways in which folk voices effectively deal with problems.

The most important thing Wideman does in *Damballah*, however, is to describe the black intellectual-writer's arduous movement back

toward the black community and black culture. Wideman understands from his reading of other black writers and from his
interaction in the commmunity that the intellectual-writer is not
necessarily an outsider, as he is often depicted in the mainstream
modernist tradition. He also now fully understands that black
culture is rich and substantive and that the black intellectual can
both benefit from it and play a role in developing it. But the black
intellectual has a problem because he has alienated himself, and he
must master the culture and work himself back into it. Wideman
goes further in *Damballah* than he did in *Hiding Place:* he speaks in
a black voice that is even louder and stronger, and he shows a black
intellectual, often identified as John and obviously a surrogate for
Wideman, as he seeks to move out of isolation and to play a role in
the black community.

The dedication and epigraph of *Damballah* begin the treatment of
the themes of black intellectual isolation, on the one hand, and the
pervasiveness of family and community traditions among black
people, on the other. The dedication, "To Robby" (the real-life model
for the character Tommy in *Hiding Place* and *Damballah*), calls
Damballah an attempt to send "letters" to Robby (Wideman's
brother), who was always more comfortable with blackness than
Wideman. The purpose of the dedication is not to make it explicit,
of course, but here Wideman is starting to deal with his physical and
psychological separation from his brother (which he also later dealt
with in *Brothers and Keepers*). Wideman is in Laramie, Wyoming,
teaching at the University of Wyoming, and Robby is in Pennsylvania in jail for life. But just as important as the physical separation
is the psychological. Wideman was always afraid of "becoming
instant nigger" by enjoying eating watermelon; in effect, he was
afraid of being black openly and aggressively, as his brother was. His
psychological separation from blackness made it easy for him to go
off to the intellectual world of academia, thereby largely calling a
halt to meaningful contact with his brother, family, and community.
Wideman wants the "letters" in *Damballah* to "tear down the
[prison] walls. . . , [to] snatch you away from where you are." As it
becomes clear by the end of *Damballah*, Wideman wonders whether
Robby-Tommy is the hero because he stays in the community and
rebels against oppression and whether he himself is the criminal for
escaping physically and psychologically.

The epigraph connects the god Damballah, "good serpent of the
sky," with racial and family tradition and leads into the book's

stories. It is noteworthy that *Damballah*, although made up of individual pieces, has a unity often found in modern short-story collections that is associated with such mainstream modernist writers as James Joyce in *Dubliners* and William Faulkner in *Go Down, Moses* and also with such black writers as Ernest Gaines in *Bloodline* and Richard Wright in *Uncle Tom's Children*. *Damballah* has this unity because it largely uses a clear, well-defined setting, Homewood; because it presents central themes from different viewpoints; and because it depicts the development of an authorial attitude toward the setting and subject matter (Werner 1982:35). This unity makes the book closer to a novel than to a collection of unrelated short pieces. In fact *Damballah* is formally very similar to Wideman's novels. Furthermore, in it, like other twentieth-century black writers, Wideman has used a mainstream modernist technique to present black themes.

The major themes in *Damballah* center on the folk characters' use of black cultural tradition and around the black intellectual's integration into the black community. Six of the twelve pieces in *Damballah* have a dominant focus on each theme. The pieces with a dominant focus on the folk use of black cultural tradition include "Damballah," which opens the book.

"Damballah" sees black history and tradition not as oppressive, as they are in *The Lynchers*, but as mythic resource and archetype, much as they are in Ernest Gaines's works; it shows how black American tradition is tied to African tradition and how this tradition is a river flowing back and forth in black history. Significantly, "Damballah" starts with Orion, a slave who still maintains his African culture and who is a "heathen" among the slaves acculturated in America, stepping into the river.

> He picked his way over slippery stones till he stood calf deep. Dropping to one knee he splashed his groin, then scooped river to his chest, both hands scrubbing with quick, kneading spirals. When he stood again, he stared at the distant gray clouds. A hint of rain in the chill morning air. . . . The promise of rain coming to him as all things seemed to come these past few months, not through eyes or ears or nose but entering his black skin as if each pore had learned to feel and speak. [17]

Orion symbolically splashes his upper body with "river" because the black tradition in which he is immersing himself is visceral and instinctive as well as being intellectual. Orion's knowledge of the tradition is not limited to perception through normal senses. He becomes an all-absorbing repository of the tradition.

Orion knows that he is going to die and that the "voices and faces of his fathers" will "carry him home again" (18), but he wants to agitate the flow of the tradition forward as well as let it take him back to his fathers. Orion sends the tradition forward through the young American male slave who is hiding in the trees, watching him. Later, Orion's eyes thrust the word "Damballah" (the god of family and community tradition) into the boy's chest, and after Orion's murder by the whites, the boy communicates with Damballah, as Orion tells the stories again before "the wings of [his] ghost measure out the rhythm of one last word" (25). The transmission of the tradition through ghosts is appropriate because the tradition is supernatural, not limited to the scientific and rational, in the same way that Orion as absorber of the tradition is not limited to normal sense perceptions. In *Hiding Place,* the supernatural perceptions of dreams help to guide Bess toward traditional values, and her language rituals work magic. Later in *Sent for You Yesterday,* ghosts bearing tradition are prevalent. At the end, the boy symbolically throws Orion's head in the river, where it will forever be a part of the flow of black tradition. Apart from the boy, the Americanized blacks regard Orion as crazy and want nothing to do with him. But he is connected to them by that which he has passed on through the boy and by the common tradition that they share.

"Lizabeth: The Caterpillar Story" shifts the setting from the South in the nineteenth century to Homewood in the present and shows how stories in the French family, also the family of John, the intellectual, link and strengthen the family generations. In "Caterpillar Story," interrelated stories about John French are part of the family tradition; as in "Daddy Garbage," the memory of French and stories about him tie the generations together. The tradition and the stories that transmit it are deep, rich, and convoluted, but French's daughter Lizabeth remembers that her love for French "had to begin with the caterpillar story." Lizabeth's mother Freeda repeated the stories to her, and Lizabeth now tells the stories, but the right voice and right words are needed to make the stories "real" (59–60). The tradition binds the generations in love if the stories are told right. A story is a ritual, and a ritual is magic whose results depend on the right performance.

"Hazel" is a story about the same extended family that is a good example of the way in which Wideman integrates themes of pain and tragedy with black tradition to create a black voicing of those themes. The character Hazel in the story has been forced from the main flow of the family and community tradition and into a diurnal and nocturnal nightmare by the accident that has left her paralyzed. In some instances, though, Hazel's mother, Gaybrella, tells Hazel about her grandmother Maggie Owens (69) and Hazel makes the family connections herself (71–72). Just as important, John French, his daughter Lizabeth, and Hazel's aunt Bess externally impose family unity on Hazel and Gaybrella by constantly associating with them and showing their concern. French and Lizabeth are always trying to pull them out of their isolation back into the Homewood community.

Really important here, however, is the story Lizabeth tells years after Hazel's and Gaybrella's deaths. She visited Hazel's brother Faun (who crippled her by accidentally pushing her down the steps) after he returned to Homewood and the old folk's home; she also rode to the hospital in the ambulance with him when he was dying. Lizabeth tells the story of human compassion and contrition that was implicit in Faun's words at the time of his death. Lizabeth remembers and tells the "whole story" (79), which extends beyond the accident, Gaybrella's total rejection of Faun after the accident, and Hazel's tragedy-ridden, death-focused life. The "whole story" that Lizabeth tells (and she tells it again in "The Chinaman") wrings positive lessons and examples from the pain and suffering. The stories that convey the family and Homewood lore involve tragedy and on a larger scale emphasize greater, useful positive values.

"The Songs of Reba Love Jackson" offers a microcosm of the black folk community and places the Homewood folk characters' use of and interaction with their tradition in a broad perspective. Reba, a Homewood community hero with a national reputation as a gospel singer, tells stories through her songs. Her songs speak of the black tradition, including the pain, suffering, poverty, and tragedy that are subsumed in its supportive values and beliefs; they also speak of the Homewood tradition and of the lives of all the individuals depicted in "Reba Love." Five of the nine sketches in "Reba Love" are narrated in the first person by the folk characters, who reveal the strength, faith, and belief that have allowed them to survive and live meaningful spiritual lives. The third-person sketches, which focus on the religious zeal of Reba's mother, the inner life of Reba, and the inner suffering of Blind Willie, all project the characters from their own viewpoints.

"Rashad" takes us back to the French family and Lizabeth, who centers her life around prayer and love, central staples in the black tradition. Not only can she love Rashad, the basically good-hearted son-in-law who is a dope pusher, addict, and an abuser of her

daughter; she can also develop a deep empathy for an old Viet-
namese man who apparently created the image of her granddaughter
on the banner Rashad sent back from Vietnam.

> He's probably dead now. Probably long gone like so many of them over
> there they bombed and shot and burned with that gasoline they shot from
> airplanes. A sad, little old man. Maybe they killed his granddaughter.
> Maybe he took Rashad's money and put his own little girl's face on the
> silk [of the banner]. Maybe it's the dead girl he was seeing even with
> Keesha's [her granddaughter's] picture right there beside him while he's
> sewing. Maybe that's the sadness she saw when she opened the package
> and saw again and again till she learned never to look in that corner
> above the mush springed chair. [149]

Lizabeth will pray for them all, her family members as well as the
sad little old man far way.

"Solitary," the final story with a dominant focus on the workings
of the black tradition, appropriately brings to a close the treatment
of the theme in *Damballah* because it shows Lizabeth's faith in
God, a main source of blacks' ability to survive within the black
tradition, being tested by the trials and tribulations of her son,
Tommy. On her trips to visit her son, imprisoned for life for
murder, Lizabeth begins to lose her trust in God. She begins to feel
that, if God's "grace does not touch her son then she too is dwelling
in the shadow of unlove," and if God can go to "the Valley of the
Shadow, surely He could penetrate the stone walls [of the prison] and
make His presence known" (179). Lizabeth reached the nadir of
despair one day when Tommy hugged her warmly and walked back
toward the "steel gate" of confinement. Then "she was more alone
than she had ever been while he raged" at her, blaming her for his
imprisonment (183).

Lizabeth returns to Homewood and tries to relocate herself in her
tradition. She tries to walk backward and forward on Homewood
Avenue in the footsteps of her father, her husband, her sons, all "her
men." She approaches the steps of the Homewood A.M.E. Zion
Church and almost goes in to ask God to "take her to His bosom"
(184). But on this day, even though she realizes God "had to have a
plan . . . , she could only see gaps and holes, the way things didn't
connect or make sense" (184). Lizabeth senses that she will need a
more powerful symbol of tradition than the "ghosts and memories"
of Homewood Avenue. She attempts to cross the footbridge into
Westinghouse Park, where she had been spending time since she was
a baby, but stops halfway, unable to take another step (187).

Lizabeth returns to the bar to find her brother Carl and once again takes up her search for the paths of tradition and security. She tries to see her father in Carl, to listen to Carl and "learn her father's voice again" (187). Carl comforts Lizabeth and assures her that they are going to cross into the park together. As "Solitary" ends, Lizabeth stands in the middle of the footbridge over the tracks, resisting her long-standing fear of the approaching train thundering under her feet, awaiting the chastening of a God who "could strike you dead in the twinkling of an eye. [Who] killed with thunder and lightning" (189). Lizabeth is ready to recenter herself by walking back into the traditional paths of Westinghouse Park, by finding again the values and beliefs that have sustained her all her life.

God and the sustaining traditions have been shaken substantially out of their place in Lizabeth's life, but they are not beyond the reach of her search. She can reclaim and reaffirm them. Lizabeth is hurt and confused but not lost. Wideman says of "Solitary" that, when he was writing it, he thought that Lizabeth had lost her faith, but when he looked back at the story, he saw that she had been saved (Samuels 1983:56–57).

"Daddy Garbage" asserts that traditional values and rites of human feeling persist for blacks in the most difficult situations and the most unlikely circumstances. It is also the first story to touch upon the place of the black intellectual with regard to the black community and the black tradition. In the main part of the story, which takes place in the past, Lemuel Strayhorn and John French bury a dead baby and say crude rites during a brutal winter when they certainly have no money for funeral expenses. In fact they strongly feel that, given the conditions in which Strayhorn found the baby, they cannot call on legal and community institutions for help. There are suggestions that powerful unseen and unconscious traditions guide French and Strayhorn, as French asks that the child's soul "rest in peace" and Strayhorn grunts "amen" and "sways like a figure seen underwater" (43). The baby enters into the community as French and Strayhorn lower him as gently as possible into the prescribed six-foot grave.

French's dedication to his family also manifests strong community values. Through his rough, crude manner, French demonstrates the strongest kind of devotion to his family. He goes drunkenly, raucously, and embarrassingly but lovingly to the hospital when his daughter Lizabeth has a son, and in his conduct he perpetuates family love and a sense of connection to the generations that follow him.

"Daddy Garbage" inaugurates a progressive series of portraits in

Damballah of the black intellectual who is not clearly in touch, or is far out of touch, with family and community tradition. At the beginning, the story focuses on a scene in the present where John, his two sons, and the children of his sister Shirley, descendants of the deceased French, are standing on the corner, talking to Strayhorn. John's aunt Geraldine is also there, and the scene clearly suggests community and family ties that span the generations. French and the spirit of his love are clearly present in the conversation. French acts to bring family and community together in the present. The only individual who seems somewhat out of touch is John, who thinks he remembers the dog Daddy Garbage, Strayhorn's constant companion in the days when they buried the baby. Strayhorn corrects John, telling him that he could not possibly remember Daddy Garbage because John was too young at the time. John was probably the son being born when French went to the hospital drunk, but he has part of the story wrong; he has misplaced a small link in the connection.

"The Chinaman" reemphasizes the power of traditional family stories when they are told right, but more important, it presents the first large role in *Damballah* for John, the educated, intellectual family member who lives in Wyoming. Freeda French at the beginning of "The Chinaman" must let her voice go "backward with her. . . . Talking to herself. Telling stories. Telling herself" (83). Later the narrative switches from Freeda's internal telling of stories, to May's voice telling the story of the birth of Freeda's daughter Lizabeth, to the tale of Freeda's grandchild (probably John) listening to the story in a family setting. The grandchild realizes that May must tell the story "right" each time she tells it or none of them will be real—none of their lives will be real (85). Stories center, focus, and make real, and stories range among generations and people in a nonlinear fashion, as memory (like Freeda's) moves backward and forward in tradition. "The Chinaman" approximates this movement in its form.

John went to Grandmother Freeda's funeral and heard the stories being told, that of the Chinaman among them. He felt that one had to be there to understand how the stories were right, how the story rituals worked their magic and made things real. But when John tells the story of the Chinaman to his wife Judy in the hotel room, on the way from Wyoming back to Pittsburgh, it is "stiff, incomplete" (93). The version of the story told by his mother, Lizabeth abounds with traditional beliefs and sources of support, which it ritualizes and makes real. For John, the story, which incorporates Freeda's symbolic representation of her death in the Chinaman and her certainty of it because he is in the hospital, means nothing in truth but "the silence of death and the past and lives other than mine" (95). Significantly, however, John adds that "the silence is an amen." Although John cannot tell the story well, and although it does not make the same traditional values and beliefs real for him as it does for his mother, he still tries to be positive and affirmative; he still says "amen."

"The Watermelon Story" is a perplexing piece portraying Aunt May's ritual of telling a traditional story of black faith that makes the faith "real" for her audience, but it also seems to be about the young intellectual-to-be discovering his place in black tradition. The first several pages of "Watermelon Story" show a young boy confused as to where he heard about a wino who fell through a thick glass window and had his arm chopped off while he dozed on an unsteady stack of watermelons in front of the Homewood A&P store. First, the boy believes that he witnessed the incident, but then he thinks that he dreamed it (100–01). Finally, "As he listened he heard May saying the words and remembered it was her then. May who told the story of the accident and then told him later" (103).

Shortly afterward, May takes over the story, in her voice, and tells another watermelon story that the first story brought to mind. May heard the story from her Grandpa. It is a story set simultaneously in Africa, slavery, and "Georgy" (104), with no place as a very clear locale. It is a story with both supernatural and religious folkloric qualities. An old woman and man keep the faith that they will have a child, and they find a child in a watermelon. But after all their rejoicing, the spirit takes back their baby boy. When she has related this turn of events, May has questions for her audience. "Where was all that praying? Where was all that hallelujah and praise the Lord in that little bitty cabin deep in the woods? I'll tell you where. It was used up. That's where it was. Used up so when trouble came, when night fell wasn't even a match in the house. Nary a pot nor a window. Just two crinkly old people on a shuck mattress shivering under they quilt" (107). The boy is horrified by the story of the old people and, to change the subject, asks Mary if the wino could grow another arm. She concludes "Watermelon Story" by answering that "God already give him more'n he could use. Arms in his ears, on his toes, arms all over. He just got to figure out how to use what's left."

The story of the old people is about faith tested and rewarded and then tested all over again. The point of Mary's comment at the end regarding the one-armed wino who has all he needs is that God always gives enough if one just waits on him, is patient, and is conscious of using one's resources. This point also applies to the old people in their desolate condition at the end, although their situation seems doubly hopeless.

What matters in both of the stories told by May is not the physical details but the ritual and rhythm. In the second watermelon story, May's colorful, rhythmic voice has force and effect, and it carries great conviction on the part of Grandpa and May. This second story, like other stories in *Damballah*, is a ritual that makes faith real for most of May's audience. For the boy, it seems horrifying. But both stories exert a tremendous impact on him, the first by creating the illusion that he was there and can tell his own version of the wino's accident.

The boy stands outside the traditional pattern that secures May in her faith. May is sure of the second watermelon story and is confident that she got it from Grandpa. She disseminates it with Grandpa's same strong faith. The boy is not initially sure where he got the first watermelon story and certainly cannot tell it as effectively as May can tell hers. Furthermore, the second story scares the boy and does not affirm him in traditional faith.

"Watermelon Story" does not reveal the boy's identity. Whereas in "The Chinaman" the first-person narrator takes over in the middle of the story, in "Watermelon Story" the identity of the boy remains hidden behind the third-person narrator. But since May is a prominent member of John's family, the boy may be John. One could read this story as another comment on the young intellectual-to-be trying to find his voice and place among the black community's traditions. Just as John's story was "stiff" and "incomplete" in "The Chinaman," the youngster here is confused and remains frightened and unfulfilled after he has heard May's stories. Wideman moves toward at least a tentative resolution of the black intellectual's predicament in "Across the Wide Missouri," "Tommy," and "The Beginning of Homewood," the final piece.

In "Across the Wide Missouri," Wideman deals more directly and heavily with the plight of the isolated black intellectual than he has in either "The Chinaman" or "The Watermelon Story." Unlike these two stories or any other story in *Damballah*, "Wide Missouri" focuses solely on the intellectual-writer's attempt to deal with the effects of his psychological alienation and physical isolation far from Homewood in Laramie, Wyoming.

"Wide Missouri" begins with the words, "The images are confused now. By time, by necessity" (133). The first-person narrator is not sure whether the bright, brash, self-assured movie images of Clark Gable come from *Gone with the Wind* or from other movies "flashing on and off" in his mind. The second paragraph switches the scene to the story's setting in Laramie, Wyoming, where the time is "spring which never really arrives. . . . Just threatens. Just squats for a day or a few hours then disappears and makes you suicidal. . . . spring . . . should have its own name. Like Shit. Or Disaster" (133–34). The narrator states, however, that nothing about the weather or geography has anything to do with the succession of images in his mind, "the river, the coins, the song, the sadness, the recollection." The conclusion of the linear collage of images reveals itself in the "recollection." The recollection reveals that the world-conquering cinematic image of Clark Gable at the mirror is really that of his father and forces him to "know why I am so sad, why the song makes me cry, why the coins sit where they do, where the river leads."

By the third paragraph, the narrator has revealed that the story acts to exorcise sadness and forgetfulness and reunites him with his father back in Homewood. In the third paragraph, the narrator speaks of the experience that underlies the succession of images and his sadness: "I am meeting my father. I have written the story before." He is saddened by thoughts of meeting his father and the story he has written about the encounter. From his written account of the meeting that preceded this one, the narrator hears his mother "like a person in a book or story instructing me. I wrote it that way but it didn't happen that way" (134). He has written the inaccurate, flawed story about meeting his father in which he tried unsuccessfully to describe and remember his father, and now he is rewriting the story. The intellectual-writer is trying to write himself out of alienation, trying to cover the gap between Laramie and Homewood. He says to himself that the weather and geography have nothing to do with the succession of confusing images and his overall plight, but he never confronts the inextricable link between his location in Laramie, Wyoming, and his sadness, his forgetfulness, and his writing of the flawed story.

The narrator tells another flawed, confused story that does not demonstrate a clear remembrance and knowledge of his father. The handsome father whom he loved intensely emerges from the image of the handsome Gable on the screen. But there are few signs that he knew his father intimately, that he was really close to him, could communicate well with him. The narrator's meeting with his father is blurry and very hard to bring into focus, because he finds it necessary to forget how much he loved his father, how little he knew him then and knows him now, and how far away he is now.

The narrator's stories move in slow motion or are a "blur of images" (136); the story he wrote before included "stage directions" (137), further indications of his instability and insecurity. Later he tries to assure himself that he is only "blurring . . . reality . . . in order to focus" (140). Afterward he says first that he understands "better" and then, in the next paragraph, that he understands "a little more now. Not much." His assurance to the contrary notwithstanding, he is not developing focus and moving toward stability.

"Wide Missouri" contains evidence that the narrator is perpetuating the same separation between him and his sons that exists between the narrator and his father, and through the infrequency of their visits to his father, he is making one of his sons a stranger to his grandfather. The narrator had a choice between going to hear one of his son's sing on his class's "Song Night" and going out for drinks with a "visiting poet who had won a Pulitzer Prize" (139–40); he chose drinks with the poet. He says he will ask his son to sing again, but the story leaves the impression that the opportunity has been lost.

It seems tragic for a grandson to have forgotten his grandfather because he never sees him and for him to be learning to forget things in general.

> I have sons of my own and my father has grandsons and is still a handsome man. But I don't see him often. And sometimes the grandson who has his name as a middle name . . . doesn't even remember who his grandfather is. *Oh yeah*, he'll say *Edgar in Pittsburgh*, he'll say. *Your father. Yeah. I remember him now.*
>
> But he forgets lots of things. He's the kind of kid who forgets lots of things but who remembers everything. He has the gift of feeling. Things don't touch him, they imprint. You can see it sometimes. And it hurts. He already knows he will suffer for whatever he knows. Maybe that's why he forgets so much. [140–41]

The narrator's alienation indirectly affects the next generation. Being disconnected from his grandfather, and to a significant extent from his father, the son seems to find himself isolated in a world where his deep, sensitive feelings have no outlet, so that he suffers.

The narrator's problems in this story begin with his failure to confront the significance of place. He certainly knows that the atmosphere of Laramie, Wyoming, with its blighted spring seasons, casts a pall over the story, but the narrator will not say directly that his living in Laramie, well over a thousand miles from Homewood, imposes a physical separation that is devastating him and his sons psychologically. The black intellectual suffers here from his achievements and from the distance he has put between himself and his past.

It is also important to reiterate the point that the narrator cannot face his problem on another level. He cannot fully face the reason why it is necessary for him to blur the images of his father and their interaction in his mind when he tries to write about them. He tries to tell himself that he is doing so for some artistic purpose, so that he can focus better in the end, or that he is somehow advancing to a better understanding. He cannot tell himself about the "necessity" to confuse images, which he mentions in the second sentence, that he is protecting himself from a painful truth that is almost too hard to bear. And the self-delusion in which he is engaging will be hard to break; it is a pattern that he will eschew only after the deepest soul dredging.

"Wide Missouri" may be the most provocative piece in *Damballah*; not only the ending but the whole story is moving. Separation and alienation inspire stimulating fiction, and Wideman demonstrates that he has mastered adversity enough to give it striking creative form. The inaccurate, flawed story that the intellectual writer is creating here is well wrought. And the same beautiful paradox recurs in other stories in *Damballah*. In "The Chinaman," for example, Wideman portrays the writer John trying to find an effective voice with which to capture the folk traditions, as many of the other characters already have, and seeking to establish a comfortable relationship with the traditions. Wideman is readily distinguished from John because he is projecting his imagination into folk life and is splendidly rendering folk voices using folk culture to deal effectively with the problems of black life.

In "Tommy" Wideman takes a different perspective to explore John's plight as the intellectual-writer isolated in Laramie. John's brother Tommy, on the run from the law in Pittsburgh, seeks refuge and succor from John in Laramie. The story is adapted from one of the "Tommy" sections of *Hiding Place* and is adapted to *Damballah*'s context. The main addition is several pages at the end in which Tommy is at John's house, talking to him.

> "You don't think you can prove your story [about the murder]?
>
> "I don't know, man. What Indovina [one of the people involved] is saying don't make no sense, but I heard the cops ain't found Chubby's [the man murdered] gun. If they could just find that gun. But Indovina, he a slick old honky. That gun's at the bottom of the Allegheny River if he found it. They found mine. With my prints all over it. Naw. Can't take the chance. It's Murder One even though I didn't shoot nobody. That's long, hard time if they believe Indovina. I can't take the chance. . . ."
>
> "Be careful, Tommy. You're a fugitive. Cops out here think they're Wyatt Earp and Marshall Dillon. They shoot first and maybe ask questions later. They still play wild, wild West out here."
>
> "I hear you. But I'd rather take my chance that way. Rather they carry me back in a box than go back to prison. It's hard out there, Brother. Real hard. I'm happy you got out [of Homewood]. One of us got out anyway."
>
> "Think about it. Take your time. You can stay here as long as you need to. There's plenty of room."
>
> "We gotta go. See Ruchell's cousin in Denver. Get us a little stake then make our run."
>
> "I'll give you what I can if that's what you have to do. But sleep on it. Let's talk again in the morning."
>
> "It's good to see you, man. And the kids and your old lady. At least we had this one evening. Being on the run can drive you crazy."
>
> " . . . get some sleep now. . . . we'll talk in the morning."
>
> "Listen man. I'm sorry, man. I'm really sorry I had to come here like this. You sure Judy ain't mad?"
>
> "I'm telling you it's OK. She's as glad to see you as I am. . . . And you can stay. . . . both of us want you to stay." [172–73]

The dialogue makes plain that John is out of touch with Tommy and his reality and is incapable of helping him. One indication is the discordance of John's more formal language and Tommy's colloquial speech. The formal, grammatical pace of John's words reinforces his failure to understand fully the urgency that impels Tommy, an urgency reflected in the start-and-stop, quick, practical rhythm of Tommy's speech. Also, the advice that John gives Tommy is well intentioned, bringing John to the verge of tears, without being helpful. Thinking about it, taking time, and resting may prevent the western cops from playing Wyatt Earp and Marshall Dillon for a while, but such "reasonable" actions will not help Tommy deal with a legal system that will not treat a black man reasonably and fairly.

Another talk in the morning will produce no results that are better. And certainly it is no solution to stay with John and his family. The truth is that nothing John can tell Tommy, no matter how level-headed and well conceived, will help him.

Tommy is an accused, soon-to-be convicted murderer who faces prison. John is also in a precarious position. John has lost touch with his home environment and with the realities of black people in that environment. His advice to Tommy almost implies that Tommy will be treated by the law in the same way as a white man. Such confusion of reality is almost as bad as anything that has happened to Tommy. Perhaps a comparison of the brothers' predicaments is suggested by the fact that Tommy sees "too many faces in his brother's face. Starting with their mother and going back and going sideways and all of Homewood there if he looked long enough. Not just faces but streets and stories and rooms and songs" (174). Tommy can see and feel John's reality and place in family and Homewood tradition better than John can.

"The Beginning of Homewood," the last piece in *Damballah*, depicts John merging the intellectual and folk voices by drawing upon black storytelling tradition to approach his brother Tommy and black cultural tradition. John is writing a "letter" (193) to Tommy after he is in jail; the letter and the story that contains it are unfinished, flawed, like the story in "Wide Missouri." The narrator says: "Rereading makes it very clear that something is wrong with the story." And since the story and letter "never got sent . . ., there is something wrong about the story nothing can fix" (193).

May's voice started him on the story as he sat wondering "why I was on a Greek island and why you were six thousand miles away in prison and what all that meant and what I could say to you about it" (194). Separated by a greater distance from Homewood and his brother than from Laramie, he heard Aunt May's voice, and it prompted him to think about his connections to Tommy. Through the "cries of [Greek island] sea birds," he heard May's voice "singing Lord reach down and touch me" with the Homewood African Methodist Episcopal Church Gospel Chorus. He had been "trying to tell [the story] for years" (195), and he wanted to connect the rebellion of Sybella Owens, his family's first black progenitor in Homewood, to the rebellion of Tommy, who had struck out against the dead-end life that had developed for his generation in Home-wood. But he had problems with his feelings of "guilt [and] responsibility"; he "couldn't tell either story [of Sybella or Tommy] without implicating [himself]." He feels implicated and responsible because he has run away from Homewood and the heart of the black experience, while these two relatives in family tradition, one distanced in time and one close, have rebelled against injustice. The sounds of May's voice and the gospel chorus, however, both resonating with the strength of black tradition, are helping him to tell the story, agonizingly.

The narrator begins an intellectual meditation on Sybella's escape from slavery and first free morning, but the gospel chorus and the voice of Reba Love Jackson cut in on him again and will not let him "dwell" (198) on his intellectual version. The voices of May singing and of Bess telling the folk, family version of Sybella's story also interrupt his meditation on the story. And he hears himself "thinking the way May talks." The ritual of the folk story is definitely influencing the narrator.

The reason that May's story is such an effective ritual and has such a powerful impact on the narrator is that her voice and storytelling technique represent the working of the black tradition in microcosm.

> I heard her laughter, her amens, and *can I get a witness,* her digressions within digressions, the webs she spins and brushes away with her hands. Her stories exist because of their parts and each part is a story worth telling, worth examining to find the stories it contains. What seems to ramble begins to cohere when the listener understands the process, understands that the voice seeks to recover everything, that the voice proclaims *nothing is lost,* that the listener is not passive but lives like everything else within the story. Somebody shouts *Tell the truth.* You shout too. May is preaching and dances out between the shiny, butt-rubbed, wooden pews doing what she's been doing since the first morning somebody said *Freedom.* Freedom. [198–99]

May's voice and story go around and around, backward and forward and sideways, like the black tradition. They are not linear; they lack the finality of movement from beginning to end. As the white world moves more linearly, emphasizing successive triumphs, May's voice pulls black life into the movement of black tradition, where it can benefit from the multiple depths and swirling currents of that tradition, all of which appear unified to anyone acute enough to see the unity. May's voice and black tradition can indeed recover everything for black people—all the valuable knowledge and experience garnered over the centuries. "Nothing is lost."

The narrator reaches an understanding and appreciation of

Tommy, and it is important for him to present it in the story. Tommy has stayed in the community, a community with diminished opportunities for Tommy's generation, and has tried to make a life there. In some ways, little has changed between the times of Sybella and Tommy, but they had the nerve to run away, to rebel against slavery and the roles prescribed for them. The narrator ran away also, but his running was no rebellion and set no example for others. Before living life in the community where he really interacted with and influenced others, the narrator slipped away through a kind of intellectual and literary passing that benefited only him. Tommy and Sybella are less a part of the community's centering, conservative traditions than are some others, but they go further and draw from a radical stratum embedded a little more deeply in the tradition: they rebel. The narrator is neither centered more conservatively nor connected to tradition by his more rebellious actions.

The narrator receives great help from May and incorporates her voice and technique as an integral part of the story, but he finally tells the story of family and community tradition and connection himself. In the last several pages of "Homewood," May tells part of the story, incorporating positive values of the black tradition, and the narrator tells part from his viewpoint. On the next to last page (204), he says that the story could end there, but May's voice pulls him along further. The narrator finally successfully completes the story and sends the "letter" to Tommy inside the final version. He finished the story in his own voice, with his own interpretation, his own special message to Tommy.

The book thus has a hopeful ending. The narrator does not tell a "stiff, incomplete" story as in "The Chinaman," or remain confused and helplessly sad as in "Wide Missouri." The narrator, John, moves closer to Wideman; he submerges himself in the tradition to the point where he can tell the story of Tommy and Sybella in his own folk-influenced voice and can face and creatively shape his own life decisions.

In *Damballah*, Wideman achieves a more uniform black voicing of contemporary and historical black problems than he did in *Hiding Place* and begins to shift back toward a focus on the black intellectual and his place in the black community. The characters are frequently speaking in their own folk voices, as in *Hiding Place*, but the difference is that the folk voices successfully project solutions to problems from the beginning and do not become bogged down in a mainstream modernist psychological alienation, as do Bess and Tommy in *Hiding Place.* In *Damballah,* Wideman is further from the stream-of-consciousness technique, with its internal focus, and is thus more removed from mainstream modernist form than he has ever been in his literary career.

The most thought-provoking aspect of *Damballah,* though, is Wideman's treatment of the intellectual quest. The intellectual-writer John is struggling for rapprochement with the black community and tries to project a voice deeply imbued with black cultural tradition. "The Beginning of Homewood" indicates that John has made great progress in his quest. Wideman himself has, of course, focused his literary imagination on the black cultural tradition in both *Hiding Place* and *Damballah.* John's closeness to Wideman gives *Damballah* a greater impact than it would have otherwise. Wideman extends this intellectual quest in *Sent for You Yesterday* (1983).

Sent for You Yesterday

The Intellectual Voice and the Movement toward Postmodernism

Sent for You Yesterday (1983), the last book of the Homewood trilogy, is transitional, like *The Lynchers* at the end of the early books stage. It marks the shift from Wideman's presentation of black life in a voice and from a perspective that draw heavily on the black folk to a representation of black life that uses a *black* postmodernist intellectual voice. Doot, the black intellectual in *Yesterday*, hears the kinds of folk stories to which John the intellectual listened in *Damballah*, but unlike John, he must create his own postmodernist subjective version of black tradition, centered on black music, in order to relate to the tradition and to make himself useful to the community. In *Yesterday* this process constitutes another progressive step for Wideman's black intellectual: he wants to serve the community, which anticipates an even stronger commitment from *Reuben*'s intellectual. The intellectual has absorbed the black tradition and has returned to the community in *Damballah*. Now the question is how he, the intellectual, with his mind and training, can be of practical help to the community.

Yesterday presents a black voicing of postmodernism that allows the black intellectual to interpret the strength and supportiveness of the black tradition and to serve the black community. *Yesterday* implies a knowledge on the intellectual's part that black tradition, particularly its oral rendition, is a subjective fiction, a statement which sounds tantamount to renunciation of the tradition, but it is not. The intellectual cannot dispense with his knowledge that all conceptions of reality are highly subjective and fictional. Nevertheless, he affirms the black tradition and the community it serves by creating his own fictions about the tradition that emphasize its depth and richness and make him useful to the community. Doot's fictions represent commitment to black tradition and black people on a subjective, creative basis that he can accept.

In his fictions, black music is a unifying structure in an indeterminate black experience. Music orders and makes sense of things where there is really only ambiguity and emptiness. Music functions at an abstract level even better suited to the intellectual's purpose than words.

Doot differs from Cecil in *Hurry Home.* Cecil is in the modernist tradition because he confusedly, even unconsciously, creates fantasies that he thinks will change reality. Doot, on the other hand, is a postmodernist because he very consciously and purposefully constructs subjective fictions that serve his intellectual needs, keep him attuned to black tradition and black people, and make him useful to the black community.

The fictions in *Yesterday* combine to create an intellectual myth. "Myth" is an appropriate term because Doot develops from his fictions an overall account of black essence and spiritual origin in a mythic sense. Doot's myth is intellectual less because of any intellectual content than because of the method he uses. He is an intellectual interpreting black experience through a highly subjective method that is peculiar to an intellectual, a method for interpreting experience that the black folk would not understand. In this respect Doot differs from John in *Damballah*. John's intellectual voice distances mainstream modernism and merges with the black folk voice. Doot's postmodernist intellectual voice is foreign to the black folk, but at the same time it incorporates the black tradition and the needs and interests of black people.

The postmodernist open-ended approach to reality frees Wideman's intellectual to be an intellectual and also completely releases him from the pessimism of dead-end mainstream modernism. Doot's postmodernist approach makes it easy for him to have freedom to explore as an intellectual and to serve black people at the same time, because postmodernism involves no presupposed, almost insurmountable pain and pessimism to work through.

The postmodernist approach also releases Wideman to explore complex literary form again, because the form is no longer associated with a mainstream modernist tradition whose dead-end pessimism can seriously complicate portrayals of black triumph and survival by means of the black cultural tradition. As a result it is easier for Wideman to speak in a black voice.

The intellectual myth is a subjective construction different from anything in the black folk tradition. In its actual working, however, the myth is not totally separable from the folk tradition in *Hiding Place* and *Damballah*. In both cases, black tradition is continuous, moving circularly, backward and forward, in all directions. Doot definitely begins to see the animating, unifying spirit of music transferred back and forth over the generations. It is ever alive in the past as a repository upon which those in the present can draw; at times when the spirit abates in the present, it flows back to its repository in the past, waiting to be drawn upon later. Doot wants to carry on the black legacy, to play an important role in the continuity of community, but he must do so from an intellectual base with which he is comfortable. The intellectual must be himself and be a part of the community too.

Doot as a narrator is similar to Jim Kelly, the narrator in *Of Love and Dust,* as Wideman describes him: he is both a character within the action and an omniscient narrator (Wideman 1978a:76–77). Sometimes Doot takes over the narrative in the first person; at other times he speaks as an omniscient narrator. But he is a first-person narrator at the beginning and at the end, and he asserts his first-person presence in the second section, "The Courting of Lucy Tate," as well. He creates the most abstruse fictions when he drifts farthest into his omniscient posture. Participating as he does in the surface actions of the story as well as in the depths of its essence, Doot can be a part of the folk community in the present, as it tries to invoke the folk spirit of the past, and he can also create the fictions and overall mythical reality that sustain him as an intellectual.

The epigraph to *Yesterday* stresses the continuity of life and tradition through people. Past lives continue through those in the present. Those in the present depend on people in the past to "live [their] lives to the fullest." In the final analysis, Doot will try to link himself to the forward and backward flow of tradition manifested in human lives.

The short part of the book that precedes section 1 is entitled "In Heaven with Brother Tate"; it is a short fiction about the practice of black improvisation and transcendence of problems before the full account in the book. "In Heaven" shows Brother, in heaven, describing to someone else a nightmarish dream about a train that made him "fraid to open [his] mouth for sixteen years cause I knowed I'd hear that scream," and if he screamed, he would be "gone" (11–12). Brother and his companion are drinking wine and sharing nightmares, and the overall tone is light, although Brother's nightmare is surely deadly. Because he is in heaven, first of all, Brother demonstrates that he can rise above the reality of the dreadful nightmare. But the comic way in which both participants describe the horrific nightmare also demonstrates an ability to deal with very fearful reality without being consumed. Doot will be tying himself into this tradition of improvisation, through words and especially music, in difficult circumstances as a way of maintaining life.

In section 1, "The Return of Albert Wilkes," the first-person narrator, Doot, uses some of the first fifteen pages or so to establish his past and present physical place in the Homewood community and to connect himself physically and spiritually with Brother Tate, who is central in the intellectual myth that Doot creates throughout *Yesterday.* Brother stopped talking when the narrator was five years old and died when he was twenty-one, and Brother gave him his scat-word name, Doot, in his grandmother's kitchen. Doot was a surrogate for Brother's son, about Doot's age, who died tragically in a fire at roughly the time when Brother stopped talking. Doot is "linked to Brother Tate by stories, by his memories of a dead son, by my own memories of a silent, scat-singing albino man who was my uncle's [Carl's] best friend" (17).

Doot then focuses the narrative on a time when "I am not born yet" (17). Here he can recreate some of the physical details from what he has actually seen and experienced in his own life and can get some from stories he has heard; moreover, he is starting to move toward the more deeply subjective and creative fictions that will become prominent later in section 1.

Brother and Carl, as boys, are going through the Homewood

streets, looking for Carl's daddy, John French. Freeda French has told
Carl to find John French because Albert Wilkes, French's friend who
is wanted by the police for murder, is back in town, and she wants
her husband safely close to her, away from Wilkes. Much of the
description is straightforward and concrete, but some of it is abstract and begins to merge into the surreal. Doot describes his
grandmother Freeda's view of the world, for example. One day, prior
to the time when she had sent Carl out to look for her husband, she
was washing dishes and saw a peculiarly shaped bubble on her hand
that mirrored the colors of the rainbow.

> My grandmother Freeda had been just a girl then. In that other room, that
> other world, enchanted by a soap bubble. She remembered its exact shape
> now. A long watermelon blister of soap quivering between her thumb and
> finger. Something had broken the spell, made her look away and the
> strange bubble had burst. She'd never been able to recall what had
> distracted her from the little soapsuds' trick. But something had made her
> look away, and in that instant the bubble had popped. Gone before she
> could whisper her wish, set it free. She couldn't remember what had
> pulled her away, but it continued pulling, drawing her past the edges of
> herself. Since that day, whenever she looked away from something, she
> was never sure it would be there when she looked back. Alone in the
> downstairs of the half house on Cassina Way listening to dishwater gurgle
> and burp down the sluggish drain she was afraid they would never return,
> not the girls [her daughters] sleeping at the top of the steps, not the man
> [her husband] nor the boy [Carl, her son] she sent to search for the man,
> not even the boy's white shadow or the shadow of herself, that dreamy
> part of herself just beyond the edge, not afraid to look away. [31–32]

Freeda has a strong creed of God and family, but this creed is "never
stronger than the voice tearing her away" (33).

Doot projects a fiction of Freeda's life that portrays her as seeing
herself living in a strange, unfulfilling world that will not let her
contemplate and enjoy life's beauties and possibilities before something distracts her and they disappear. This uncertainty and
insecurity in her life is stronger than anything, even her creed of
God and family. Clearly, this picture of the world differs from that in
Hiding Place and *Damballah*, where characters use religious beliefs
and storytelling rituals to keep themselves within black tradition.

Doot's fiction begins the creation of the essence of an experience
in the black community that, in the final analysis, is animated and
realized by black music. Music makes the images, the rainbow
colors on bubbles, stay intact so that people like Freeda can con-

template and enjoy them. Music puts things in their place and makes them stay there, thereby eliminating the insecurity and uncertainty. Music is the language that, in a postmodernist context, brings certainty and security to an indeterminate experience. In the overall context of his myth, Doot will not be saying that black life and tradition are impoverished; rather, he will be choosing one specific aspect of the tradition, black music, to convey its sustaining essence, an essence he will cloak in his fictions. Many of the characters will not see secular music as a carrier of a spiritual, unifying quality (Freeda, for example, hates blues), and they certainly will not share the intellectual fictions that he will create.

The larger myth develops more fully as the narrative slides into omniscience; after Doot calls attention to himself with his first-person narration at the beginning of the last long passage quoted above, he does not again speak in the first person until early in section 2. In the meantime, the story is to all appearances omniscient as it speaks of Brother and Albert Wilkes. First, Brother is an ugly albino who, although irritating to Freeda at times, is a very important part of her life. She feels his presence even when he is not physically close. Thinking about Brother makes her think of her dead mother Gert. Freeda will not like and agree with the things for which Brother ultimately stands in *Yesterday,* but he is central to her existence and to Homewood. The reasons become clear later in the book and particularly in section 3, entitled "Brother."

Albert Wilkes returns to Homewood after a seven-year absence. He shot a white policeman because of a woman and fled. He was *the* Homewood blues musician, and he played a few notes before he left.

> One more time. Somebody had named the notes, but nobody had named the silence between the notes. The emptiness, the space waiting for him that night seven years ago. Nobody ever would name it because it was emptiness and silence and the notes they named, the notes he played were just a way of tipping across it, of pretending you knew where you were, where you were going. Like his footsteps in the snow that night. Like the trail he tramped that was covered over as quickly as he made it. [55]

Wideman is projecting another fiction about the reality of the black experience, and central in this fiction are black music and the black musician as symbols of unifying structures in an ambiguous, indeterminate black reality. This quotation shows that Albert is an integral part of Homewood and its blackness and cannot escape them, no matter what he does or how hard he tries to flee from them. He is lost when he is away from Homewood. But there is a more important point here, too. It is that the music structures and gives meaning to the "emptiness," the "silence" of experience, just as the music would structure Freeda's experience and take her above her feeling of emptiness and insecurity. Experience—the black experience, too—will always be silent, but the music is a way of "tipping across it, of pretending you knew where you were, where you were going." The emptiness and silence would overwhelm Homewood if Albert and his music did not exist. These ideas suggest a view of the indeterminacy of reality that undercuts the ability of language to organize and unify. Music is, perhaps, more abstract than language, and is consequently more suited, for the black intellectual at least, to carrying the abstract and indeterminate but rich essence of the black experience and tradition.

A section of the narrative that begins one paragraph after the last passage quoted above (55–57) focuses on the ambiguity of language and the questionable authenticity of stories as to who saw Albert first when he returned. The account plays on various meanings of the name Bucket of Blood (a bar in Homewood)—as a place where black men draw each other's blood; as a bucket of "bloods," or black people; and as a bar is sometimes full of "bloods." It is clearly implied that the various stories of who saw Albert first when he returned are harmless but at the same time apocryphal. As previously noted, certainly not all stories are apocryphal as in *Yesterday*, but traditional stories in the myth developed here lack the quality of magic ritualization that they have in *Hiding Place* and *Damballah*.

When Albert returns, he finds Homewood both familiar and unfamiliar: he "believed he held every detail of Homewood exact in his memory, but now he wasn't sure" (57–58). Furthermore, "[he'd] been here before, [he] knew this was going to happen" (59). Albert embodies the spirit of music in Homewood. When he is away, his memory of his spiritual place—his repository in a sense—dims, and Homewood also becomes dim and inanimate. But also when he is away, the memory of the music, for Albert and for Homewood, vaguely recalls the essence that sustains life.

Once Albert is back in the Tate's house, where he used to live, he can go to the piano and "begin playing the seven years away" (60). He can create his reality through the music, can play away the "emptiness," the "silence." But his music sometimes does more. It shapes the universe: as he plays, there is a "moody correspondence between what his fingers shape and what happens to the sky, the stars, the moon." For his best friend, John French, Albert's music makes it clear that beauty is strikingly present in the world, and it harmonizes his interaction with his wife, Freeda (81–86).

French feels that maybe "all Homewood coming apart" (67) and hopes that Albert's music can put it back together again. French hopes that it will be like the "good old days when Albert playing and Homewood hanging on every note" (68). Albert's music can indeed reconstruct Homewood and animate its existence again. As previously noted Homewood is sustained by the memory of Albert's music. Albert's memory in his absence is like a ghostly presence that keeps people going, and the people themselves are, in Albert's absence, ghosts moving around in their proper and predictable places, ready to be brought back to life. Albert and the spirit of his music must return if the ghosts are to live and if Homewood is to be revived. The following passage illustrates the strength of the narrative.

> You could roll over in Hell and if there's a clock on the wall and it's saying four-thirty in the afternoon you can bet they doing what they always do that hour in the Bucket of Blood. Nobody forgets, nobody worries, nobody gets tired. Look around. Everybody busy, everybody in place. Albert Wilkes gone seven years but if he walks through the door this afternoon he'll know who to speak to, what to say, where to stand and nobody'd hardly notice. Like he never left. Like he got a brother . . . and that brother could hang around in Homewood and save Albert's place till Albert gets back. Almost see him sometimes. Albert's shadow moving around in the Bucket of Blood like a natural man. Nobody bothers him, nobody gets in his way. Wouldn't be the Bucket of Blood if they did. Wouldn't be Homewood if you couldn't hear Albert's music when you walking down the street.
>
> So it wasn't so much a matter of missing Albert as it was a matter of having him around when he's gone. All those shadows and pieces of Albert moving through the bar but you can't call him over, you can't tap him on his shoulder because it's just that ghost holding his place till Albert gets back. Albert Wilkes around like that fine piano music around and it's not a matter of being gone but being here and being gone both. Like a tune you can start and hum some of but you can't get the best part, can't hum it through and finish it like Albert would.
>
> Nobody this morning looks like they miss Albert Wilkes and nobody believes they might be the one missing tomorrow. . . . [But] if you counted back, used your toes and fingers a couple times to count the years, these bloods in this bucket all be down home, be in the cotton

patch sweating for Massa. If you counted ahead a short minute, touched
your fingers and toes two or three times apiece all these boys be dead. All
be lost as Albert's ghost haunting these walls if Albert don't come back.
[70–71]

In one sense, Albert's movement, in and out and back into the
community, parallels the flow of the black tradition: it moves back
and forth and around and around, sustaining and supporting the
black community throughout time, just as the end of the passage
quoted suggests Albert's importance in the past, present, and future.

In the passage quoted above, French says that Albert was unnoticed, although his "shadow" was in the Bucket of Blood, and later
Albert tells French that, since he has been back, it is "like I was
invisible" to people (78). Not until he sits down and starts playing
the blues on the piano at the Tate house does someone notice,
namely the police, who break in and shoot him to pieces.

Albert's music is the life-renewing spirit of Homewood, and it also
allows him to focus his own reality. But with the gift of his music
that is the saving spirit of the community, with the gift of music
that articulates his identity and is generally a source of insight and
revelation, there comes a bitter fate of recognition. Albert embodies
the core of the tradition in the black community, but in that role he
attracts the deadly fury of white oppression, which is the major
harmful force that, directly or indirectly, the supportive tradition
allows black people to withstand. Those who carry on the music
and the tradition after Albert also bear the burden of suffering and
death because of their gift. It is almost as if they, as carriers of the
essence of black life and tradition, must die, must sacrifice themselves before the life and tradition can continue. But just as Albert
and his music live in people's memory when he is gone, they live
through others when he is dead and continue through others when
they die.

Wideman in section 2 starts to draw Brother Tate further into the
narrative as a central symbol who will carry on Wilkes's legacy. In
the section "The Courting of Lucy Tate," Brother and his adopted
sister Lucy Tate were at the Tate's house, listening to the music, when
the police broke in and killed Albert. Lucy says Brother was "fidgeting
beside me and moving his fingers like he's playing a piano so I said
[to Albert], *play.* And Mr. Albert Wilkes did" (102). Albert's name did
not come back to Lucy until he was "in the middle of the music,"
but the music was so good that "didn't nothing matter but the
music." Obviously, Albert's music influences Lucy here, overwhelm-

ing her, making her feel that nothing else mattered; she will be one of the strongest promoters of his legacy. Brother, however, standing beside Lucy and mimicking Albert's movements, will be the most direct and important carrier of Albert's legacy.

Having been deeply touched by Albert's music, Lucy as a thirteen-year-old passed the influence on to Doot's Uncle Carl. When Carl went into Lucy's house he "landed in the footprints of Albert Wilkes," and he felt that Lucy and Brother lived in "a haunted house full of chain-dragging, piano-playing ghosts" (98). Albert's spirit symbolically presided as Lucy and Carl went through the rites of their initiation into love. The unifying symbol in these rights was a piece of Albert's skull that the police had shot from his head and that Lucy had saved. The bone fragment was like a "rare, white pebble from the grimy hillside where the trains run" (104). This image hints at Albert's significance in the context of a sometimes bleak, dangerous black reality (trains signify danger in all of Wideman's fiction about the Homewood experience). The scene in which Lucy put the piece of bone in Carl's hand had an almost mystical quality. Carl and Lucy made love for the first time under Albert's spell, starting a lifelong, mutually supportive relationship.

The relationship between Carl and Lucy was not complete, however, until Brother became an inseparable part of it, when he brought Lucy's cryptic love note to Carl: "[Just because] I showed you that bone don't make you grown up" (108). Maybe Lucy's meaning is ironic: perhaps symbolic acceptance of Albert did indeed make Carl grown and ready to be a true lover. Carl was at first embarrassed when Brother sat watching, "ready to grin" (110), as he tried to remember the note without taking it out again and to decipher "the million words." But Brother did not grin. He scat sang as Carl tried to understand the note. His scat singing, a form of music like Albert's piano playing, helped Carl comprehend the experience with Lucy and calmed his insecurities. As Brother scat sang, "It was all right. It was the three of them now. No secrets." In a sense, Lucy's note is the language of life, the language of grown-up experience. It is cryptic and unclear, just as Albert found the meaning of his experience to be unclear and just as Lucy's experience with Carl was unclear. Brother was an important part of the relationship because his scat singing, like Albert's piano music, named the silences and ambiguities and imposed significance and meaning on life. Brother thus plays a very important role in the community that comes to fruition in section 3. Here he connects with Carl and Lucy to create a microcosm of the black community with its unifying spirit of music. The actual "meaning" of the note does not really matter.

As in *Hiding Place*, Wideman does not romanticize the black community but shows it successfully coping with its problems through its traditional spirit as manifested in Brother. The symbolic community of Brother, Lucy, and Carl succumbs to dope addiction after World War II. Brother, however, was at least two-thirds of the solution to the problem. Although Carl committed himself to an institution (as did Eddie in *A Glance Away*) and still relapsed from time to time after his release, Brother quit taking dope and made Lucy stop. Brother stopped taking dope "like magic [because] Brother was different from other people" (154). Brother was carrying the saving spirit of Albert Wilkes, the saving spirit of music. As an embodiment of the powerful, traditional, saving spirit of black people, Brother is playing a more directly practical role in solving the problems of the black community than did Albert, his predecessor. The narrative is working from Albert, to Brother, to Doot. The more practical working of the saving tradition, transmitted through music, becomes important as the story approaches Doot's role in the present. Again, the full account of Brother's ability emerges in section 3.

Brother's embodiment of the traditional musical spirit that he got from Albert is reinforced by his seemingly spontaneous recreation of Albert's music in 1941, when he was twenty-one years old. Brother, with Lucy, had watched Albert play, but Brother did not start playing until Thursday. On Saturday he reproduced Albert's music at the Elk's Club. According to Carl, it was not Brother playing; Carl would not look "to see *who* it was" playing the piano (91). Carl does not know that the traditional spirit, originally invested in Albert and now invested in Brother, was producing the music. The movement of the musical spirit and its ability to transform are magical, somewhat like the transformations produced by language ritualization in *Hiding Place* and *Damballah*.

Carl does realize, though, that Brother "said what he needed to say in his own way"; he "didn't need words" (121). The scatting musical sounds, which, as shown at the inception of Carl and Lucy's relationship can clarify and order life as music does, and the playing of the music that Saturday night, were enough. But after the death of his son Junebug in a fire, Brother stopped saying even the few words that he had rarely spoken and also stopped playing music. Doot's intellectual myth expands to incorporate the change in Brother after Junebug's death in the "Brother" section.

As in the first section, Doot in section 2 asserts his physical presence as a first-person narrator and a participant in Homewood affairs and also creates the intellectual myth from the omniscient point of view. Early in section 2, he says, "I was born about six months before that evening in 1941 [when Brother played Albert's music]. So already I was inside the weave of voices, a thought, a way things might be seen and be said" (93). Between 1941 and 1946, when Brother was playing, Doot may have heard Brother play. In addition to making himself a part of the Homewood community from birth, Doot is tying himself to Brother, to Albert Wilkes, and to the musical tradition that Albert represented. (Brother placed Doot in the musical tradition by giving him the musical scat word "Doot" for a name.) Carl also tells Doot that, one night when he was a baby and the music was playing, Doot was patting his feet and Lucy got him up to dance. But Doot pulled away and danced by himself, as Brother was "scatting with the music like he always did" (119). Brother's scatting and the music gave Doot his own sense of special movement and expression much as Brother and Albert Wilkes had. Doot is very much a physical part of the community in the past and present and is also closely tied to Brother Tate and Albert Wilkes as cultural figures in the community. At the end of section 2, Carl invites Doot over to Lucy's to form the third part of a threesome, to take dead Brother's place in the old relationship.

As an omniscient narrator, Doot creates the surreal fiction about the power and persecution of Junebug in section 2. At one point, there is an obvious break from the traditional kind of community story told in *Hiding Place* and *Damballah* and an emphasis on the abstract, abstruse fiction of the intellectual. Carl is telling Junebug's story, but Lucy decides that "she'll leave Carl's story alone. He doesn't need her helping words, her amens, her reminders of dates, of names. She's telling it [Junebug's story] to herself. Her way" (124). Doot is present and involved in the conversation, but the omniscient narrator takes over and develops Junebug's story from the deep recesses of Lucy's mind. Lucy's refusal to listen to Carl's traditional community call-and-response story represents a comment on the relative place of such stories in *Yesterday*.

Lucy's story ties in with *Yesterday*'s intellectual myth about the legacy of the black tradition. Junebug, who extends Brother's legacy, was born enclosed in the caul of special vision, which reflects his ability to make revelatory statements to the black community, and he makes only humming musical songs similar to Brother's scatting. But his brothers and sisters fear his white appearance and his difference, and they kill him by dousing him with kerosene and pushing him into a fire. Junebug's persecution differs from the oppressive violence that kills Albert, but both of them die as a result of being special black people with special gifts. Brother's creative spirit is seemingly stifled and the black community blighted after Junebug's death. (Brother stops playing music, and Lucy, Carl, and Brother succumb to dope addiction.)

Junebug's story is a part of the intellectual myth that focuses heavily on the tragedy of the black community and shows horrible realities of black life severely testing the ability of the traditional spirit of music to provide the strengths, insights, and revelations able to sustain and revivify the community. The story of Junebug's mother, Samantha, offers another example of tragedy. Samantha's life is deeply infused by the rhythms of music, and she has the nationalistic vision of strengthening the race by populating the world with all the black kids she can. But Samantha has Junebug, an albino, by Brother, although she never before associated with a light-skinned black man, and Junebug's persecution and killing by his brothers and sisters shatters Samantha. She ends up in the Mayview insane asylum, where Lucy visits her and watches her disintegrate all over again. The end of Section 2 focuses on the tragedies of Junebug and Samantha and on the problems of Carl and Lucy after World War II. It remains for the intellectual myth to develop the specifics of renewal in the black community in the "Brother" section.

In the 1941 part of the section on Brother, the omniscient narrator projects the essence of the train dream for Brother: the dream became a vision of his legacy from Albert Wilkes, made plain his responsibility for the legacy, and illustrated the effect on people of his special gift. In the dream, Brother was Albert "coming back to Homewood . . . until the lights went out . . . , the doors slammed . . . , the bodies began crashing into him . . . , the screaming began" (160). "Later, the train wheels sounded . . . like somebody telling the same sad story over and over again in the same tired voice and the wheels couldn't do nothing but keep on telling the tale" (161). But also in the dream, the music that Albert and Brother played gave people what they needed to make life "still and calm"

(163). Brother shared with Albert the reality of a horrible, sad black experience, but the music that he and Albert created brought order to this experience and revealed ways in which people could sustain themselves.

The dream encompasses other elements of tragedy, but in it the tradition, the spirit of music, persists and allows the general community to continue while permitting Brother to distance his horror and accept his responsibility. In the dream, Brother's vision of his personal connection to Albert as a special person, almost a prophet who must bear the burden of sacrifice, made him go to the police and inform on Albert, with the result that Albert is killed. ("Albert Wilkes's life was hanging on him like a skin to be shed, a skin he couldn't shake off, so it was squeezing, choking all his other lives. It would kill him forever if he didn't shrug it off, so he ran from the living room and up Tioga to Homewood and Frankstown and said to a white policeman he'd never seen before that Albert Wilkes was back" [163].) Albert's coffin, however, shrinks to the cradle of a white-skinned child being rocked on a spring morning. Brother and Junebug are obviously born out of Albert's death and carry on his traditional spirit and legacy.

In 1946, after the death of Junebug, the horror of the train dream returned, and Brother grew cynical about everything, even the music he used to play. Brother did, however, still sing to Junebug *"to save his life"* (170). He told the dead Junebug a little story in his mind.

> Listen, son. Listen, Junebug. It all starts up again in you. You are in me and I am in you so it never stops. As long as I am, there's you. As long as there's you, I am. It never stops. Nothing stops. We just get tired and can't see no further. Our eyes get cloudy. They close and we can't see no further. But it don't stop.
>
> Brother tasted soot. He wondered if that was the taste of a lie. Had he lied to his son? What bright, shining day ever came? [171]

Sadly, Brother realized that he should tell someone about the horror of the train dream, which will return repeatedly, but knew he would not because he would never say anything else.

In 1962, at the time of his death, Brother becomes fully mythicized and spiritualized. Sixteen years after Junebug's death, after having distilled the reality of this death and that of Homewood life, Brother floated high above Homewood like a spirit. Brother had seen everything he needed to see, and said everything he needed to say, so all that was left was to play "the scare game [with the train] one more time [before he died]. Teach Junebug wasn't nothing to be afraid of. Teach them all [in Homewood]" (181). Brother's spirit at the time of his death had risen above the horror of the train dream. His spirit triumphed and left a message for Homewood and a place in the spiritual tradition for Doot to fill.

Much of the passage entitled "1970" takes place in the present. In this section, Wideman takes the story of Brother from the surreal level of Doot's fiction to a more mundane level closer to the daily life of the Homewood community, where Doot can pick up the tradition Brother represented and can move toward assuming an activist role in the black community. Lucy is central in this transition because she has indeed been well "courted," not only by Carl, but also by the Homewood tradition as it is represented in Brother and in Albert's music. "Albert Wilkes's song so familiar because everything she's ever heard is in it, all the songs and voices she's ever heard, but everything is new and fresh because his music joined things, blended them so you follow one note and then it splits and shimmers and spills the thousand notes it took to make the note whole, the silences within the note, the voices and songs" (189). Lucy has a deep feeling for the way in which the tradition orders black life and at the same time exposes all of its rich and wonderful parts. Although she lacks the special gift of Albert and Brother, she has absorbed the tradition more meaningfully than Carl.

Lucy initially opened the way so that Brother, like her an orphan, could be a part of the Tate family and consequently of the Homewood community. It did not matter to Lucy that Brother was an albino without a name. If the Tates loved them both, she would accept him into the house and be his big sister, although he was older than she, and they would have a family.

Lucy is also responsible for finding and revealing a way in which Brother had a symbolic impact on the community, although this impact was less clear and direct than his scatting and piano playing. She finds pictures that Brother drew of the older generation of Homewood people—Mr. and Mrs. Tate and John and Freeda French— in which they are young again and dominate the scene on the Homewood streets. Like his music, Brother's drawings have the power to animate and revivify.

> [Looking at his drawings] was like listening to people who can really sing or play an instrument. Doesn't matter what they play or sing, they put you in it and carry you away. Carl's mother and father, Albert Wilkes, the Tates. All the good old people and good old times. She could see Brother's

hand, pale as the paper, moving across each sheet. Like the magic hands of the old-time healers. See him laying on his white hands and see through them to the old Homewood streets, the people coming to life at his touch. [194–95]

The power invested in Brother was a magical one with a sustaining influence on people during his time, although Homewood declined somewhat. Someone else endowed with the same magical touch can bring Homewood to life again.

Most important, Brother, like the old folks, set an example of not giving up. Brother and the old folks were "solid, real." They made Homewood: "That's why Homewood was real once" (198). Brother was also like the old folks because he controlled his destiny: he chose how he wanted to live, and even how he wanted to die (199). (There was no physical reason for Brother to die, since the train did not hit him. And as Brother stated in the "1962" subsection, he did die when he wanted to, after he had proved an important point.)

Doot has been constantly asking about Brother, and near the end, he is sitting in Brother's chair in the Tate house, ready to become a player in the tradition, a conveyor of the spirit. The stage is set for him: "The piano, spotlighted on an empty stage, waits for someone to materialize from the dark corners of the room and play" (200). On the last two pages of the book (207–08), Doot emerges from the shadows of the stage, the "pattern of light and darkness" surrounding his face (200), to assert his "I am" posture again. It would seem that any remaining shadows of doubt about his role have been dispelled. "Black Music" is playing on the radio. The spirits of Brother and Albert enter to support Doot with more music, and Carl and Lucy give him vocal support. Doot takes center stage: "Everybody joining in now. All the voices. I'm reaching for them and letting them go. Lucy waves. I'm on my own feet. Learning to stand, to walk, learning to dance" (208). As indicated by the title "Sent for You Yesterday, and Here You Come Today"—the song that Lucy got him up to dance to when he was a baby (207)—Doot is a day late but still on time.

In the "1970" subsection, Lucy is insightful and especially important because she shows Doot and Carl just what Brother's legacy in Homewood is. Still overall, the core story in *Yesterday* is plainly a myth about the black community developed through the fictions of an intellectual individual and a postmodernist form. The open-ended postmodernist form of *Yesterday* is Wideman's most complex creation since *Hurry Home*, but the form does not carry the stigma of mainstream modernism and its dead-end pessimism, with which Wideman struggled before he could draw on black tradition to achieve a black voice. Furthermore, in the postmodernist tradition the intellectual can soar and still serve the black community. This individual is not necessarily isolated or alienated from the community as he is in the modernist tradition. The resulting freedom is ideal for Wideman as a writer. In an interview with Wideman in 1982, the interviewer asks, "How would you describe your concern with form at this stage of your development?" Wideman answers:

> Form for me is an adventure. . . . This goes for all kinds of expressive activities. I think it's an Afro-American cultural inheritance. "Dr. J." plays basketball very well, but he also used basketball as a means of self expression. He has mastered the techniques. So not only do you see basketball (the game) being played, but you see "Dr. J." Ideally, that is how I would like to play basketball, the way I would like to write a novel, and do anything else. Very frankly, writing is a form of display, as well as a mastering of craft. And I think any writer, particularly this writer, can allow the desire to display himself get a little bit out of hand. Until you really learn the fundamentals, until you are very, very good, you can't afford to do too much jiving around. But once you get those fundamentals mastered, then, the whole point is to jive around. You can call it experimentation, or you can call it ringing the changes, or you can look at it as doing what Afro-American musicians do. I value spontaneity, flexibility, a unique response to a given situation. Creating little boxes for yourself and dancing out of them. Getting too close to the edge but then recovering like the heroes of the Saturday matinee serials. That's excitement. These are the things that draw me to writing in general. I don't want to know exactly where I am going. I want to get there and still deal with it. I want to set up situations that make me work in ways that maybe I have never worked before in fiction. [Samuels 1983: 50–51]

In *Hiding Place* and *Damballah*, Wideman successfully explored and described the qualities inherent in black folk culture; he accepted a much more balanced view of the black community. He focused solidly and securely on the things important in the community in the eyes of those who lived there. Intellect and imagination were no longer places where he hid from blackness; indeed they became places where he embraced blackness. He could now proceed to the kind of "display," obviously similar to postmodernist "play," of which Wideman speaks in the interview.

Viewed in this perspective, *Yesterday* is a very fine book. Wideman has come home to and is comfortable with his black experience and community as he was not in *Hurry Home.* At the same time, his improvisation ("ringing the changes") in the context of fictions and myth is wonderful. Creatively, Wideman effects a true synthesis in his career, distancing modernist pessimism and using postmodernist concepts very well. In *Yesterday* he strikes out in a new direction. Like Wideman, Doot has come home to the community and is ready to improvise intellectually while carrying on the community tradition as Albert Wilkes and Brother have done in the past.

Reuben

Postmodernist Potential Realized

In *Brothers and Keepers* (1984), the first of Wideman's recent books, he finally and fully establishes his allegiance to the black community. In *Reuben* (1987), the next book and the first novel in this stage, Wideman takes his comfortable, secure role as writer-intellectual loyal to the community as a starting point to pursue *Sent for You Yesterday*'s postmodernist approach even further. The writer-intellectual loyal to the community can explore ways of portraying that community creatively however he wishes. Postmodernism is a good approach for this purpose because it does not restrict possibilities for the black community as much as modernism; Wideman does not have to cut through modernism's dead-end pessimism and gloom to achieve a black voicing of black life and black problems. And he can subvert postmodernism's resignation and inactivity, which may undercut necessary social and political action in his black characters and in the black community. Neither Wideman nor his character Reuben accepts the resignation that accompanies the theory.

In *Reuben*, Wideman exploits postmodernism's wide open possibilities. He takes improvisation and skillful writing that we see in *Yesterday* to a higher level of experimentation while achieving a black voicing of postmodernism. In the process he experiments, improvises, and "displays" himself as a writer (Samuels 1983:50–51). In so doing Wideman portrays a set of characters different from those of the Homewood trilogy although he continues to use Homewood as a setting.

As in *Yesterday*, fictions evolve into a myth in *Reuben*, but this time the overall myth draws heavily on African cosmology, African tradition, and an African myth of origins. Wideman acknowledges Robert Farris Thompson (1983) "for *Flash of the Spirit* and its exposition of Kongo cosmology," and the fictions and myth of the character Reuben obviously draw heavily upon the second chapter of Thompson's book, "The Sign of the Four Moments of the Sun: Kongo Art and Religion in the Americas." Reuben's myth is partly a cultural construction, centered around African and Afro-American rituals and beliefs, that he uses to focus himself in the black experience, but it is also a fictionalized personal history that he uses to enforce upon himself timeless, ideal values that will support him in serving the black community.

Wideman has said that Reuben is a " 'kind of a god or spirit' trying to 'hold his community together, prop people up, keep them going' " (Davis 1988:26). This statement links Reuben's function with that of black tradition in *Hiding Place* and *Damballah* and even more clearly with the saving spirit of music in *Sent for You Yesterday*. Although he is very different in many ways, Reuben embodies Homewood's saving spirit, as do Albert Wilkes and Brother Tate, but he is, very generally, like Doot in being an intellectual. One might regard Doot's development as having come to fruition in Reuben because he is an activist in the community; Doot is preparing himself to be one at the end of *Yesterday*.

Although Reuben is a central figure in the community because he is a lawyer to whom poor blacks take their cases, the characters do not consciously regard him as a spirit, but they do sense that his presence is ubiquitous, magic, saving. For example, Kwansa Parker, a poor black woman who comes to Reuben after her boyfriend attempts to win legal custody of their son, has the feeling that she has

been "seeing him her whole life. . . . [Reuben was] part of Homewood like the A&P's big window, the pillars of the bank, the music
pounding from Dorsey's record store, the sweet burnt grease smell
floating half a block on either side of Hot Sauce William's rib joint"
(2). She cannot clearly recall Reuben's trailer, in which he conducts
his law practice, but she has the impression that the trailer has a
magical, protective quality.

> Trailer sits in the vacant lot behind Hamilton over near the school.
> Wonder is nobody run him away from there. I mean, yu can't just plop no
> trailer anywheres you wants now. Guess it's too old to bother with. Guess
> it looks like it's just growing out the ground like the rest of the weeds
> over there. Naw, I ain't never heard nothing bout no color. Think it was
> blue last time I looked. Kinda sickish, peeling, light blue. They say one
> time under the moon it was blood red. They say it shivered like silver or
> gold when it stood Saturday afternoons up on Homewood Avenue. Course
> no police gon bother it. Reuben's the law, ain't he? [6]

Wally Carter, Reuben's friend who is a University of Pennsylvania
graduate, a former basketball player, and now a college basketball
recruiter, immerses himself in abstraction and insensitivity. Wally,
however, also has a deep feeling that Reuben's ubiquitous presence
saves him by giving him some meaningful contact with the world
outside himself. In the following quotation, Wally wonders how
Reuben could have been an indispensable part of his life while he
was in school in Philadelphia inasmuch as Reuben was obviously in
Pittsburgh, in Homewood, the whole time.

> Wally has memories of those school years that don't make sense without
> Reuben around. If not Reuben, somebody like Reuben talking to Wally. Or
> maybe it was more a matter of missing Reuben, the way you miss your
> water after the well runs dry. But you got to have the water first, don't
> you? Like wouldn't he have to know Reuben *before* he could miss him.
> You had to have a thing at least once or you couldn't miss it, could
> you? . . . When Wally deserted Homewood for college and all that knowl-
> edge, he'd left Reuben behind so how could the old man be in both places.
> He hadn't been. No way. . . . Wally had never spoken to Reuben till he
> returned from the university so he couldn't have carried Reuben's con-
> versations to Philadelphia. Couldn't have missed him because he didn't
> know him yet. [113]

The point Wally cannot make is that Reuben's timeless, enlighten-
ing, revelatory spirit allows him to grasp some important things in
his life and prevents him from becoming more isolated and destruc-

tive. Reuben also connects things and makes sense of them for the entire Homewood community.

Reuben is an intellectual like Doot, but his intellectual myth encompasses ideas, whereas the term "intellectual myth" is used in *Yesterday* because of the process and method by which the intellectual constructs the myth and not because of its primary content. Reuben has well-defined ideas about reality, life, and the black community that the intellectual myth in *Yesterday* only suggests from time to time. The inspiration for part of Reuben's thinking is the photographs of the English-born nineteenth-century photographer Eadweard Muybridge. At the beginning of the third chapter of *Reuben*, Reuben gives his postmodernist interpretation of Muybridge, who he thinks captured an essential aspect of reality that eludes words. Words are only "seen as real by weak creatures like [Reuben] who pretended they were authors of the universe" (61). Words therefore do not convey reality. Muybridge thought, however, that he could catch the essence of motion, the essence of life, if he used his cameras to freeze people and animals in various series of frames. But Muybridge's cameras never caught motion, never caught and defined the impulse that propels life. Motion and life are as undefinable, as irreducible, as reality. Reuben through Muybridge also sees that time is undefinable. The concepts of beginning and end, of movement and progress, and of cause and effect cannot shape, define, and reduce time to its essence.

If reality, life, and time are unknowable, undefinable, then the meaning of existence is an illusion constructed from various fictions about reality, life, and time. But at this point, Reuben dismisses Muybridge and refuses to withdraw from participation in the affairs of the black community. Reuben knows that there is life in the balck community, although as an intellectual he believes that he can know only the illusion and not the essence of that life.

Blacks in the community see only the illusions imposed by fictions, but they still perceive the quality of their lives in distinct ways. When the illusions are painful and oppressive, they are no less burdensome and harmful because they are illusions. Those imposed directly or indirectly by the dominant white society are often oppressive, restrictive, and harmful, and as a legal practitioner, Reuben wants to take actions that create positive counterillusions of movement, progress, and change in black community life.

An important point about Reuben is that he is an activist in the black community; to become an activist, he overrides the sense of resignation created by his belief that reality is only a subjective fiction. Doot prepares to be an activist at the end of *Yesterday;* Reuben is the community activist brought to realization.

As an intellectual-activist, Reuben is a mythmaker like Doot; in his fictions of his personal history that constitute part of his myth, Reuben develops the necessary values, approaches, and attitudes that will prepare him to take constructive actions in the black community. For Reuben, these fictions are empowering because they give him the strength, direction, and focus to do his work. These fictions are set against the restricting, imprisoning fictions that the white society imposes from the outside on Reuben, on other black individuals, and on the black community. Reuben's fictions allow him to create illusions of progress, change, and movement over time in the black community and thus to help the community.

In essence, Reuben believes that, although blacks, like everyone else, may be living an illusory existence, he and the black community must escape the controlling fictions imposed by the dominant white society. The black community, and particularly Reuben as the intellectual-activist, must create and live its own sustaining illusions and not those imposed by white society through its debilitating fictions. Sustaining illusions of existence are all that the black community has, and Reuben's fictions at least prepare him to take the actions in the community that create these illusions.

Reuben is creating positive illusions and slipping out of imprisoning fictions. To parallel what Reuben is doing, Wideman is displaying his agility in form and is writing himself in and out of fictional boxes that he creates. In *Yesterday,* parts of the narrative, particularly near the end, invite the reader to deconstruct them, as Reuben at the same time tries to deconstruct fictions that would restrict him while keeping freedom in fresh, sustaining illusions. Wideman allows the text's fictions, its meanings, to deconstruct or assume different meanings and references so that Reuben will not be trapped and hurt by them. The combination of Reuben's vigorous ideas, which sometimes sound as if he has been reading postmodernist literary theory, and the form to capture Reuben's thoughts and activities make this perhaps Wideman's most demanding book. Such improvisational writing on the edge, "Getting close to the edge but then recovering," pushing his ideas and his medium further and further, is a large part of writing's central activity as Wideman sees it (Samuels 1983:50–51).

Reuben's legal steps create the counterillusion that helps prevent blacks from being trapped in white society's fictions. Reuben regards the steps of Muybridge's photographs, which captured the "illusion of motion" (16), as similar to the steps he takes in his law practice to help Homewood blacks such as Kwansa. The legal steps create a "fiction of motion," of movement, progress, and improvement, just as the sequence of Muybridge's photographs created the illusion of motion's essence.

Through Reuben's meeting with Kwana in the latter part of the "Kwansa" chapter, the first chapter, Wideman emphasizes the point that Reuben, the legal practitioner and intellectual-activist, must work with other blacks to deconstruct negative fictions if he is to construct positive counterillusions. After Kwansa has left Reuben's trailer following her first legal conference, Reuben feels the need to call Kwansa back to his trailer immediately and "go over the familiar territory [of her story] until it wasn't familiar anymore, till it was a starting place unlike anyplace either of them had been before. Unless they started fresh they'd be caught up in one fiction or another, and that fiction would carry them wherever it was going. And its destination would have nothing to do with where they needed to go" (17). This is a symbolic action in Reuben's mind; he does not call Kwansa back to go over her story. But the point is still made.

Reuben then thinks about the process that he must go through personally before he can take action: he must "stoop to the black-magic tricks" of myth and mythic ritual to accomplish his goals. Part of the process that Reuben must go through before the end is ritualization, the repetition, of the mythic accounts to himself, and part is a physical ritual of sacrifice and love associated with the accounts.

Reuben starts developing his myth by creating a fiction of African genesis, the story told by the "old Dogon sage Ogotemmeli" (18). Reuben wants the fiction to begin the process of getting him to the place where he can take constructive action in "this bad dream of Homewood and lost children and mothers grieving." But Reuben's fiction depends too much on underlying assumptions that he can understand and specify the movement of time, which Reuben earlier conceded is irreducible and undefinable, like reality and life. Reuben tries to create a fiction from a "chain of events, one after the other," and he becomes lost in Aretha Franklin's song "Chain of Fools." He pessimistically speculates that maybe the overall mythmaking process will not work, that he cannot escape the chains of restricting illusion: "Maybe nobody ever escapes. Maybe it's boxes within boxes within boxes cutting off your air. But you smile anyway when you hear of crazy coincidences or when they happen to you" (19).

Reuben's pessimistic speculation ends in hopeful perplexity about unexplainable coincidences, but he plunges into total confusion near the end of the chapter. He must then tell a story, create some kind of myth, to pull out of confusion toward a position where he can take positive action.

> Reuben tugged the gold watch from its nest below his heart. Eleven forty-seven. Coincidence? All numbers had their secrets, but this one didn't even try to be coy about what it was hiding. Eleven once. Then eleven again as the sum of four and seven. What do you have: eleven twice. Four ones equal four. East, west, north, south are the four points of the compass. The four corners of the world. Four moments of the sun. A circle connects them. Everywhere, everything, perfection.
>
> He smiles at the tired ivory face of the clock cupped in his hand. . . . The whole world . . . , including the intersection of Homewood and Hamilton, where lunch will be waiting in a tiny, four-table Muslim restaurant eleven steps from the corner. [22–25]

Reuben's fiction provides the illusion of "perfection" because of its "trickology and numberology" (to use Bess's terms in *Hiding Place*), because of its ritual performance of language. It at least takes him beyond the false assumption that caused his confusion in the Dogon fiction: the assumption that he could define time, break it down into its "chain of events." The language ritualization that he finally accomplishes belies any assumptions about knowledge of the essence of reality, life, and time. The ritualization produces results magically by arranging numbers into unusual relationships that produce the illusion of "perfection" in the world; knowledge of the "secrets" of reality, life, and time is not actually important here.

Just as important, Reuben's fiction moves him toward a strong cultural myth. The phrase "four moments of the sun" refers to Thompson's *Flash of the Spirit* (108–09), where it alludes to continuity and indestructibility in Kongo cosmology. On the basis of this cosmology, Reuben is developing a myth of the self and black culture that will center him and will give him the continuity, consistency, and endurance to help black people. At the end of the chapter, Reuben has reached the point where he can further develop a myth that will lead to action through powerful personal fictions of sacrifice, love, purpose, wisdom, and commitment.

Wideman entitles chapter 4 "Thoth," the name of the ancient

Egyptian god of wisdom, learning, and magic. By giving the chapter this title, he connects Reuben to Thoth in the African mythical tradition. Reuben will have to display wisdom, learning, and magical power like those of Thoth to do his job for black people in Homewood.

In "Thoth," Reuben draws upon the powers of Thoth to fashion a connected fiction, charm, and ritual that will help him to do his job for Kwansa. Reuben begins by setting the fiction in an indefinite time frame. His mother was "born in another century" (64), and his own birth and that of his twin brother "happened too long ago." His birth happened, but he was also "just there, where he'd always been, under the rock of darkness waiting." Significantly, Reuben does not start with a "chain of events, one after the other." He will not try to order, define, and reduce time, because he can never penetrate time's essence. He will make a charm and use it to perform a ritual that will magically mold him into time's cycles. It is a magical and symbolic ritual similar to that which appears at the end of chapter 1. The result is a fiction that produces the illusion of "perfection"; he creates an important symbol that in the overall myth will inculcate an ideal love, sacrifice, and caring that will inspire his later actions. He concludes the ritual with a magic incantation to Thoth.

After Reuben talks about the twin brother who was taken from him, he describes the charm and its shaping.

> At the bottom of his watch a brass charm was attached by the thinnest gold wire. Reuben fingered the bullet-shaped object. The wire passed through a hole in the bullet's nose, then through a loop on the watch. To see the charm Reuben had to pull his watch from his vest pocket and to check his watch he had to drag out the charm. Since the watch was linked to a chain and the chain pinned inside his vest and his vest fastened around his midsection, the container of his heart, lungs, liver, et cetera, Reuben sometimes thought of the charm wearing him. Conceived of himself as an elaborate headress flowing from the pointed helmet crowning his brother's skull. Because the charm was an image of his brother. Yes. If you looked closely, you'd see that the object decorating Reuben's watch was not a bullet, not a miniature whistle or pencil but a man, severely stylized, African style, all torso and brow and arching crown. Only the barest suggestion of arms, little amphibian nubs held stiffly at its sides, and stubby, elephant-toed feet. Years of rubbing, of talking to the little statue with his fingertips, had streamlined its features. He'd fashioned a man. . . . Honed for motion, speed, a charge of bristling energy compressed under the conical cap. [64–65]

In the latter part of the quotation, Reuben goes through the magical acts of rubbing and talking to the charm that make it an image of his brother, but the quotation also describes a larger ritual and the associated constructive myth. Reuben performs the ritual acts that incorporate the image of his brother's life and the irreducible rhythms of time into his visceral being. The myth that is developing will show that Reuben possesses timeless, ideal love and sacrifice.

The narrative subsequently confirms the ritual and Reuben's timeless commitment to his brother in the myth. At some indefinite point—"In a dream or vision or during one of the extra lives he grew more certain he had lived, the longer he lived" (66)—Reuben learned that his brother was in jail, and he "mourned his lost brother from that day." Part of the ritual of sacrifice he developed then was to keep the image of his brother's life with him at all times. At night, Reuben performs ritual penance by putting the watch chain around his neck like a noose and tying himself to his brother's timeless grief and the endless cycles of time. There are "circles within circles within circles linked over his bony chest, which rises and falls almost in time with his brothers" (67). The developing myth says that there can be no beginning and no end to the love and sacrifice that Reuben must show for his brother.

Reuben's myth seems complete as his magical incantation connects the power of Thoth and his timeless commitment to his brother with his responsibility for Kwansa and with action in Homewood affairs. "O Thoth, Mighty Moonglow Maker, Great Inkspotter and Inkblotter, the one who puts the Tick in my Tock, be with me this morning. You and anybody else willing. Do your best. Help me with this child's [Kwansa's] business. Reuben's watch beats in his vest pocket. Telling time, the job he must do" (68).

Reuben's task is not complete, however. As he makes another charm more directly symbolic of his commitment to Homewood, Kwansa, and her son Cudjoe, voices assail him, shouting negative fictions—"Mountebank. Charlatan. Fool. Witch doctor" (71). The voices are "all of Philadelphia laughing him out of existence again." Reuben's myth is not yet capable of holding back society's destructive fictions, which negate his existence and his ability to act on behalf of the black community to create constructive illusions of life. Reuben must return to his experience in Philadelphia before he can attain the more practical focus he needs in his myth. The

Philadelphia experience will contribute to a myth with a more practical emphasis in terms of black American racial relations. The myth develops in the fiction of Flora that Reuben creates in chapter 5, "Flora."

Flora, a beautiful, goddesslike, light-skinned black woman, was a prostitute with whom Reuben had the briefest of love affairs while he was surreptitiously learning the law as a factotum for University of Pennsylvania fraternity members who were studying to be lawyers. The white fraternity members arranged the affair between Reuben and Flora so that they could secretly watch Reuben, a diminutive, deformed man, make love to the healthy, beautiful Flora. But the brief affair became a highlight of Reuben's life. Reuben immediately fell in love with Flora, shared his intimate feelings with her, and promised to take revenge on the fraternity boys who had used them both. The fraternity members overheard the conversation and decided to punish Reuben and Flora by raping Flora and making Reuben watch. Their cruel spectacle is interrupted, however, by a fire, apparently started by Flora's erstwhile black lover Dudley Armstrong, that kills Flora and leaves Reuben unconscious after he has fallen from the second-story window. Obviously, this fiction has a much more specific time reference, namely to Reuben's younger years at the university in Philadelphia. The specifics of American racial prejudice and injustice are also present in the brutal racism of the white fraternity members, who humiliate Reuben and cause Flora's tragic death.

The fiction gives Reuben's love affair with Flora a timeless quality and contributes to the myth.

> She [Flora] is a sinuous spine of hills rhythming the horizon. He thinks of earth shapes, what lives and dies in spaces those shapes contain. How many times has it happened? With this woman. In cities by the sea, on high, windy plateaus, in Memphis, Timbuktu, New Orleans, Thebes, sand dunes, a field of rushes, seasons swirling so there is a blur, the best of all of them—hot sun and fall colors, the perfume of spring, snow's sparkle and weightless drift—when his lips graze her cheekbones the first time again. [84]

Reuben then feels that "he is not in a room in West Philadelphia. He's not anywhere else either. They've slipped from time."

The Flora fiction projects values and attitudes that are timeless in their depth and do not force Reuben to attempt the impossible task of ordering and reducing the stages of time's movement. The important point, however, is that the Flora fiction is both timeless and specific enough to move Reuben to action in the context of the black Homewood community and the problems confronting Kwansa. The fiction silences, temporarily at least, the hostile voices with their overtones of black American racial stereotype that shouted Reuben out of existence at the end of "Thoth."

The Flora fiction gives Reuben a combative attitude that he needs; the main qualities underlying both the brother and the Flora fictions are love, sacrifice, and human responsibility, though. Near the end of the chapter, Reuben promises Flora that he will hurt the white fraternity boys and take revenge on them, and Reuben tells Wally that the story of his encounter with Flora is one of both love and hate. Wally, who has set himself apart from others in what he calls "abstract hate," does not understand what Reuben means, but Reuben is only talking of the antagonism toward white people that would give him the necessary commitment and purpose to do his job for black people like Kwansa. Some degree of antagonistic feeling is necessary from a practical standpoint to silence racist fictions and carry out actions that create positive illusions for blacks in a white, racist setting. The Flora fiction prepares Reuben by giving him a practical, specific example of oppression that the fiction of his brother did not give him. After Wally leaves, Reuben again takes out the charm that is symbolic of his work for Kwansa and Cudjoe and the folder with information about the case; this time the hostile voices do not assail him (95).

The extent to which the Flora fiction reflects actual events in Reuben's life is unclear, but it need not be clear, and Reuben need not have any traceable life history. Reuben resides in the confused, shadowy world of his intellect, one which presents him only with illusions and not with the substance behind them; consequently, actual life events ordered in sequence are not very apparent or important to him. What is important to Reuben, though, is for him to help black people, who have definite perceptions of the quality and reality of their daily lives, Reuben's ideas about illusory existence notwithstanding. What Reuben really needs, then, is not a clearly articulated life history but strong attitudes and values developed out of a mythic structure. These attitudes and values will force him to action, no matter how he feels about the uncertainty of his own physical existence. The Flora fiction is part of the myth that gives him these values and attitudes.

Chapter 7, "Reuben," focuses again on Reuben's uncertainty about the reality of his life, which he would define, if he could, in terms of its motion, movement, and progress: "Is motion progress, the fiction of one Reuben making headway toward a particular place on a particular day?" (126). But (as Reuben knows from his association with Muybridge) motion, life, and reality defy synthesis and definition.

> No matter how many cameras, a different Reuben in each frame, a slightly altered pose, a separate reality. Amazing, isn't it. How protean the simplest gesture. And each pose real, definitive, if we possessed a means of capturing it. If we could see everything. If we bore God's eye in our foreheads. A paradox, an irony. To slow things down, we must click the shutter faster and faster. Do you see what I mean? Less light. More and more pictures as the time scale shrinks. The shutter blinks a million times an instant yet it's not fast enough. Motion defeats it. Motion slips through the net no matter how fine the weave. Motion the sum of all the tiny inchings forward but something greater, irreducible. Fantastic. Don't you agree, Mr. Reuben? [126–27]

As in "Thoth," Reuben then dismisses his intellectual query and uncertainty and tries to move ahead with his work.

Mythic penance and sacrifice will translate into an act of commitment and responsibility that will give Kwansa the illusion that there is progressive movement in her life. Most of the remaining part of the chapter shows Reuben focusing himself for his task through the fictions of Flora and his brother. Both of them are tragically lost to Reuben, and he must use all of his energy in penance and sacrifice for them.

Reuben traverses the gap between his intellect and its mythic values, on one hand, and Kwansa's life in the Homewood community, on the other, through the ritual process of his law practice. "His spit-shined shoe returns to the sidewalk [from the step of the courthouse]. It gleams impersonally. No face in its depths stares back at him. If the shoe fits . . . , if it doesn't touch the floor when you scoot back into a chair . . . , you are Reuben. You wear it. You hobble off toward Stanley's Bar and Grill [where you can make the actual legal compromises to help Kwansa] (134).

The ritual actions and the illusions he creates make the difference; Reuben's reality and the real substance of what he does with the law are not important. There is still "no face" showing itself in Reuben's shoe. That is, he still cannot see or know the true reality of himself, but he is Reuben because he is acting for Kwansa, and she has a perception of him and what he is doing for her.

A hostile white fiction interrupts Reuben's wavering trek toward his goal of action on Kwansa's behalf, however. In chapter 10, "Mr. Tucker," the white society actually attacks Reuben by charging him with impersonating a lawyer (it is never clear what Reuben's official legal credentials are) and threatens his existence with a cruel fiction in the newspapers about imposture. Reuben attempts to escape the fiction first by refusing to read the story in the newspaper and then by claiming to himself that "none of it ever happened" (195). But Reuben's other escape acts illustrate different techniques.

Wideman, and Reuben, deconstruct the form and theme of the narrative. Reuben talks to Wally and tries to avoid the newspaper story and to deconstruct the harmful fiction about him at the same time. Part of the technique consists of presenting dialogue between Reuben and Wally out of chronological sequence. Wideman gives stagelike directions: first, "[*And before this exchange leading to it*]," then, "[*Back to the above, Reuben speaking again*]" (196). Later, the narrator and subsequently Reuben break up the scene between Reuben and Wally to remove Reuben from the newspaper fiction altogether.

> The band begins playing again. A serenade of the sounds of the bar, the city, the country, the whole eggshell earth. The eye of a funnel closes in on itself, spinning like a whirlpool, lines of force like ribs whirling in its white maw. A device in old movies for dissolving from one scene to the next. The picture on the screen whorls down a drain. Darkness gulps the swirl of actors, actresses, the elaborate set topples too, tumbling, wiped out. Script reads: *Dissolve to . . .*
>
> Reuben makes it a ranch. Home, home on the range. Blue Wyoming sky, gray waves of sage. Stars and stripes crackle like tinsel in a fabulous sky. Everybody's happy, wherever they are, whatever they're doing. The ranch house, the cookhouse, the bunkhouse, in the saddle riding the range, fishing, singing round a campfire, mending fence, steering the steers, daydreaming, nightdreaming, climbing a ladder of stars and bars to heaven and back. Yippee. I. Oh . . . [201–02]

Reuben uses the fluidity of reality and of the text to his advantage; it serves him by letting him out of a restrictive fiction, whereas before the fiction retarded his effectual action in the Homewood community. The feelings in the passage are conventionalized and sentimentalized, but Reuben is happy and riding free in open Wyoming space, not humiliated and restricted in Pittsburgh.

The last chapter of the book, "Toodles," reemphasizes Reuben's idea that we can capture only the illusion of reality. The last section

of the book, "And," reemphasizes this idea and also the notion that
Reuben must project himself beyond his confusing, indefinite, uncertain intellectual world and take action for blacks in Homewood.
These black people consider reality definite, concrete, and certain
and measure the progress of their lives in these terms.

The somewhat humorous language in the "Toodles" section does
not accurately convey reality. A few pages into "Toodles," we realize
that "we sit imagining ourselves imagining them [Kwansa and
Toodles talking about Kwansa's hard times]." The scene here, and
Homewood reality, is an illusion, an invention of our imaginations.
"We" are also fabrications of our own imaginations. Furthermore,
the story that the anonymous voice tells of Kwansa fighting with
Waddell, who has stolen Cudjoe, and of Toodles cutting his throat
seems to be very much embellished. (In this respect it is reminis-
cent of the apocryphal stories in *Yesterday* about who first saw
Albert Wilkes when he returned.)

"And" begins by asking us to "imagine" the whole scene. The last
few paragraphs force us, along with Reuben, to penetrate a dense,
blinding atmosphere to the place where Reuben greets and picks up
Cudjoe for Kwansa.

> Our eyes are directed by the eyes of the dwarfish man to the face of a boy
> inside the room. There is no accounting for the power that connects the
> dwarfish man's bearded face with the young face, half a head shorter. A
> beam of light fuses them. We are momentarily blinded. We see nothing
> but a luminous, smoky shaft, as for an instant we are surrounded,
> drowned by light. The sides and backs of our skulls have dropped away.
> It's scary, but seemly, doesn't hurt. If others are in the room, they
> shouldn't be. So we lose them and lose ourselves and ride the wave of
> light long enough to hear the old man say,
>   Hello. You're Cudjoe, aren't you. I'm sorry I couldn't get here sooner.
> Don't be frightened. Your mother sent me. She said she loves you and
> will see you soon and everything's going to be all right. My name's
> Reuben. I'm here to take you home. [214–15]

Part of the point in the passage is that Reuben has an unaccount-
able "power" because, as we saw at the beginning of this chapter, he
is an abiding, ubiquitous spirit in the community; but the main
point is that Reuben transcends his confusing, action-negating,
postmodernist intellectual world to act for Kwansa. *Reuben* ends as
Reuben does so. The intellectual's act represents an assertion of
faith that what he is doing is meaningful because he is making black
people happy. The act, the assertion of faith, thrusts him beyond

selfish, inactive, residence in his own private world of intellectual belief in the illusory quality of everything we can create. It thrusts him into active participation in what he knows is the illusory reality of other people, but what is important is that these people feel he will make a difference.

The black voicing of postmodernism in *Reuben* consists in the creation of fictions to develop a constructive myth of black culture and Reuben's personal history that allows him to help black people; part of the black voicing also consists in the negation of postmodernist resignation that Reuben expresses. The myth in *Reuben* is a solid, complete structure by the end. It is a myth of black culture and tradition with deep, abiding roots in African belief, ritual, and spirituality that is continuous, and it is also a myth of the timeless, enduring, constructive values that inform Reuben's life and make him a part of black culture and tradition and also a servant of the black community.

Although Wally Carter lacks Reuben's intellectual scope, he is an educated black man who separates himself from others in his own inner life of the mind; Wideman, however, is concerned to show that Wally is radically different from Reuben. He differs from Reuben in that he loves his separation and will not try to reach out to others or to help them. Wally, in fact, refuses to try to relate to anyone but Reuben, who has a special attraction for Wally because Reuben seems to make Wally's existence complete in some way that it could not otherwise be. Wally develops a fictional character ("the recruiter") and a fictional case of "abstract hate" that really describe his attitude toward white people and toward black people too for all practical purposes. "Abstract hate" comes as close as words can to describing Wally's life and existence in a world where words are inadequate to convey reality. Wally's abstract hate involves coldness, callousness, insensitivity, and isolation, while Reuben's fictions convey love, sacrifice, responsibility, purpose, commitment, and loving feeling toward others. Wally illustrates what happens when an educated, thoughtful black man closes himself off in his mind and makes an independent life there. (Wideman took an ambivalent attitude toward Cecil's somewhat similar approach to life in *Hurry Home*.)

In chapter 2 of *Reuben*, entitled "Wally," Wally shows how he likes the total freedom of his dreams and of a fluid identity. Wally's dreams are not supportive and reinforcing because they are partly the repository of tradition, as they are in the Homewood trilogy.

Wally feels certain and sure in his dreams. In one of his favorite fantasies, he abandons the disguise of an old woman and "pisses all over" everyone (34). The other extreme from placing oneself in a position where destructive fictions can trap and restrict is finding the wide open existence where one can be free and do almost anything. The world is sufficiently confusing and chaotic to permit someone who is sufficiently detached and isolated from other people to live in this way. Wally chooses this latter option for his life, but as the book shows, he pays the price of being lost with no anchor in people by which he can pull himself home. Reuben chooses to try to help black people and make himself known by his actions, and as a result he must combat the racist fictions that attempt to preserve the status quo. But Reuben's choice is much more meaningful because his reward comes in the satisfaction and support he gives other people.

Chapter 6, "The Recruiter," another chapter about Wally, reveals Wally's ideas that time is chronologically disordered and life is illusory, ideas very similar to Reuben's, but it also reveals further the details and depths of Wally's abstraction and detachment.

> Wally treats his life like a memory so he won't have to worry about what's happening to him. Since the shit was already over, since it had gone down the way it was going to go down, like it or not, he would treat what he was doing as if it was happening to someone else. Stand way back. Be sorry for the sucker. Laugh at him. No sense in worrying. Too late. And since his life was a memory, he could change it next time he played it. He could tell any lie he needed to get by. It's all in your mind. A dream made up as you go along.
>
> But if you're not there, living smack-dab in the middle of your life, then where the fuck are you? Every once in a while the question stings Wally. If your life's not a memory or a tale you concoct at will, playing it fast-forward or reverse, stopping and starting in the middle or end, if your life's more than this mix of yes or no and maybe and skipping and losing and somebody else working the dials, then who are you? A fly tracking across the dome of the [basketball] arena, a spider curled in the rafter's shadow? [102]

Wally has basically the same vision as Reuben of life as undefinable, as an illusion that he can contemplate from a distance. But unlike Reuben, Wally decides to stand clear and let life pursue its disordered course, although Wally does question his own cynicism and abdication of an active role. Wally will not make Reuben's commitment, his assertion of faith that it is worthwhile to plunge through his own doubts and concomitant isolation to make others feel their lives are better. Once Wally decides that "it [life] had gone down the way it was going down," he withdraws into isolation, to manipulate life's wide open possibilities with, if necessary, an occasional lie.

The point in *Reuben* is not that black men like Wally lack a pressing need to escape from the pressures of white society; the account of Wally's experience at the University of Pennsylvania in particular supports this point. Rather, highly thoughtful black men must, like Reuben, overcome their intellectual doubt and the burden of racism before they can relate to and help other blacks.

An extraordinary effort is required, but Reuben manages it. He creates a whole new life for himself that prepares him to participate in the lives of other blacks. He distances the humiliation of his personal experience with racism, which would make him ineffectual. Reuben gives himself only a first name and structures a mythic existence that will produce the values and attitudes he needs to spur him to action in black people's lives. The closest he comes to the horror of his personal experience is his fiction about Flora, and this fiction involves love and devotion more than anything else.

The point is not that Reuben represses personal experience but that he creatively manipulates it in a fluid, wide open world so that he can take unselfish actions. Wally Carter, on the other hand, lets personal experiences with racism force him into selfish isolation. His account of his life makes it sound far worse than Reuben's, although it is not necessarily so. The difference is the creative shape that the men choose to give their lives. Reuben overcomes intellectual doubt and what he believes is racist experience to make other blacks feel that they are progressing. Wally builds intellectual doubt and racist experience together into an isolated tower of cynicism and hatred.

The recruiter motivated by "abstract hate" whom Wally creates is really Wally, and his portrayal shows how Wally is slipping farther into self-isolation and a consuming abstraction. The creed of "abstract hate" allows Wally to commit murder in his mind, and his crime assumes such stature that it dominates him. He does not know whether he murdered the white man as he says or not. Wally labels a positive, mythic story that Reuben tells him a "lie" (107), but he cannot see that his story of "abstract hate" is equally a "lie" (the details of the recruiter's life do not completely match Wally's). The difference is that Reuben's "lies"—his fictions, his myth—direct him toward a role in black people's lives. Wally's "lie," his tale of "abstract hate," only forces him into self-consuming isolation and abstraction.

"Bimbo," chapter 9, also focuses on Wally and reveals again Wally's cold detachment from others and his absorption in isolation. Pretending he is writing letters to other people while he is jogging is Wally's way of "being in touch. . . . Learning other lives are as arbitrary, disposable, unlikely as his own . . . Letters answering his letters confirm Wally's fictions. . . . If he's wrong, it matters not. Lives he makes up keep him moving" (166–67). Chapter 9 further emphasizes the point that Wally is deteriorating.

The chapters dealing with Wally have shown a progression; in "The Recruiter" Wally slipped further into abstraction, and in "Bimbo" Wally's reality is to a large extent symbolized by the broken, useless body of his childhood friend, the popular singer, Bimbo. Wally, like Bimbo, cannot carry out any meaningful action. He cannot even help his friend Bimbo commit suicide, as Bimbo wants. Bimbo lives a horror worse than death, and Wally is so consumed in his isolation as to be useless—he might as well be dead. Images of death pervade the chapter.

When Wally and Bimbo were kids, Wally showed traces of the pitiful person he later became. Chapter 9 shows all of Wally's callous potential realized. As an adult Wally has forsaken the youthful rituals that at least forced him to have a modicum of meaningful contact with others. The game of basketball was such a ritual for Wally. But pressures of age and work have now made Wally turn to jogging, by which he only reinforces his callousness and insensitivity. At the end of chapter 10, Reuben tries to call Wally back to participation in life, but Wally is so far gone that the appeal's chance of succeeding is open to question.

The two other main characters in the book, Kwansa and Toodles, are not intellectuals like Reuben and Wally but examples of the need for saving fictions about the self and the world to create a meaningful illusion of existence. In chapter 1, Reuben feels the urge to call Kwansa back to his trailer and to rehearse her story so that some hostile fiction will not take over and carry them both where it wants to go. Reuben does not know in how many ways it would be a good idea to do so. He does not know that Kwansa's main problem is her lack of a fiction of herself and of life in general that will keep harmful fictions from the outside, indirectly imposed by white society, from devastating her.

In chapter 1 when Reuben asks Kwansa to tell her story, she

thinks that she "has no story. Her life is now. The pain sitting on her lap is her life" (5). Kwansa's lack of a story and of a self-protective fiction, much less a constructive myth that will allow her to develop values and address the needs of others, is the reason that she cannot cope with her situation better. Waddell and his light-skinned sisters can threaten her to such an extent because she feels black, ugly, and inferior. Deep down, she believes that they stand a good chance of triumphing over her. Chapter 8, "Big Mama," tells how Kwansa's grandmother unwittingly helped Kwansa to internalize the fiction of herself as bad and unworthy. Maternal love for her son Cudjoe, which is instinctual, alone saves Kwansa from destruction and makes her keep trying to do good. It is noteworthy, however, that Kwansa does have some innate quality that keeps her from suffering Wally's fate, which is worse than hers.

Wideman's very sympathetic portrayal of the relationship between Kwansa and Toodles highlights the fact that Kwansa must have a bond with another woman who has her fiction and illusion in place. Every word spoken by Toodles indicates that she has developed a fiction of self and the world that will prevent anything from hurting her. Toodles would not consciously think that she has developed a fiction, and certainly in the overall context of the book, fictions to protect the self are not as meaningful as Reuben's fictions and larger myth, which inculcate values that help him help others. But still, Toodles may be the toughest and least vulnerable character in the book, even tougher and less vulnerable than Reuben.

The narrative at the end of chapter 5 focuses on Toodles's supportive bonding with Kwansa through the lovemaking act.

> She needed to cry and Toodles's bony shoulder was close so that's where she laid her head first thing. Then her hands on Toodles and Toodles hands on her. She told the woman her troubles. And the woman kissed away her tears while Kwansa talked about Cudjoe, about wanting to be better than she was. The woman nodded, listened, undressed her gently, like you would a child, not to take anything from it, but giving it what you believe it needs, your hands unbuttoning and loosening and unpinning because it's time. Funny, because turned out to be Toodles doing the watching, the listening, the waiting, keeping her hands to herself. Toodles who was willing to let a tiny bit or nothing at all happen. Kwansa who twined with the long body, took its toes between her teeth and wouldn't let it wiggle away. [96]

Toodles bonded with Kwansa and empathetically ministered to her needs; Kwansa twined with Toodles and relieved herself of some of her pain. The book gives greatest emphasis to Reuben's act on behalf of Kwansa, but Toodles's participation in Kwansa's life gives her the female empathy she needs desperately.

Through *Reuben*, Wideman returns to a primary emphasis on a black intellectual's interaction with the black community. In his previous books, black intellectuals who were the central focus were Cecil in *Hurry Home*, Thomas Wilkerson and Littleman in *Lynchers*, and Doot in *Yesterday*. Reuben is both similar to and different from the black intellectuals in Wideman's previous books. Like Cecil, Reuben spends much time in the fantasy world of his mind, but unlike Cecil, he consciously projects fictions that bring him out of this fantasy world to take action in the black community. Reuben's sharp mind and misshapen body are reminiscent of Littleman, but bitterness and frustration do not consume him as they do Littleman. Reuben is much clearer about himself and his role in the black community than Doot; he is acting in the black community, not just preparing himself to do so, as Doot is.

Wideman's superior portrayal of Reuben reflects his awareness of possibilities after he has reassessed the black community and has described it in positive terms in *Hiding Place, Damballah*, and *Yesterday*. Wideman still understands how the black intellectual can go wrong, as his portrayal of Wally shows. Wally succeeds in cutting himself off more completely than even Cecil, who does, however, return to Esther at the end of *Hurry Home*.

One of the most important things about *Reuben* is Wideman's unveiling of new postmodernist techniques and a broader thematic range to deal with the unique role of Reuben the intellectual-activist. Wideman has stressed that experimentation is important to him as a writer. In *Reuben*, he experiments with devices that Reuben uses to deconstruct damaging fictions about him and with ways of leaving the narrative open for deconstruction by the reader. As previously noted, in his creative, deconstructive process Wideman parallels Reuben at times. Furthermore, Reuben's ideas about reality differ from those of any of Wideman's other characters. It is a significant achievement to pull these ideas together in an experimental form that is adequate to handle them and the other requirements of the narrative.

The techniques by which Wideman captures the book's fluid reality and Reuben's lofty intellectual flights probably make *Reuben*'s form the most difficult in any of Wideman's books, including *Hurry Home*. At times the narrative is hard to follow, but it is important to keep in mind that time, reality, and human existence in *Reuben* are indefinite and indeterminate. As a result, events do not always take readily recognizable forms; what is recognizable is illusory anyway. An example is a dialogue between Reuben and Wally in which the lines are designated by the stagelike directions W and R (36–37). The dialogue is set off in the text and seems to be an almost telepathic exchange. Wally is not sure whether the conversation actually happened. But given the chaotic flow of time, uncertain existence, and illusory reality in *Reuben*, one should accept the conversation as part of the way things work in the book. It is in Wally's memory and is a central element of his strong attraction to Reuben.

Wideman attains new goals in *Reuben* by achieving a fuller, more complete black voicing of postmodernism than he achieved in *Yesterday*. The postmodernist approach allows Wideman to write freely and to experiment as much as he wants, but at the same time, it allows him to be deeply committed to blackness, as he wants to be. This commitment to blackness means creating for the black intellectual a supportive, useful role in the black community. It also entails imaginative use of such black writers as Ralph Ellison and Robert Hayden; several times in *Reuben*, Wideman alludes to *Invisible Man* and "Middle Passage." In *Reuben*, Wideman's art is alive and flourishing.

Conclusion

During his career Wideman has always struggled to write as well as he can. He has continually pushed his craft to new achievements. After his early successes, he sought to reshape his artistic imagination and sensibility using influences dominate in black cultural tradition. Elements of this tradition and borrowings from other black writers entered his literary style and structure. Wideman has also sought rapprochement with the black community through his black intellectual characters. In *Brothers and Keepers,* he explored his own personal isolation as a black intellectual from the black community.

In this book I have traced Wideman's development from a narrow portrayal of the black experience that drew on the restricting forms and themes of mainstream modernism, to a black voicing of problems common to modernism and the black experience, to a black voicing of postmodernism by which he could articulate the strengths of black culture and could support the black community. In so doing I have followed Wideman through each book as he integrated the black intellectual into the black community, after he had come to understand and respect black culture and had distanced himself from mainstream modernism, which, as I have shown, often involves alienation from the community. Wideman's development takes place through three main stages: the early books (*A Glance Away, Hurry Home,* and *The Lynchers*); the Homewood trilogy (*Hiding Place, Damballah, and Sent for You Yesterday*); and the recent books (*Brothers and Keepers* and *Reuben*).

Wideman's artistically least successful book is his first, *A Glance Away.* The book is thematically highly derivative of T. S. Eliot and particularly of "The Love Song of J. Alfred Prufrock" and *The Waste Land.* Wideman was obviously trying to establish himself as a writer by merging into mainstream modernist literary tradition, but by remaining so close to Eliot's modernist expression, he curbed his development. He was certainly improvising somewhat on Eliot thematically, but still his close approximation of Eliot's pattern limited the extent to which he might explore the black experience and various artistic and creative possibilities in *Glance.*

Wideman still, however, showed an ability to innovate and experiment with the more purely formal aspect of *Glance.* In developing the modernist formal structure of the book, Wideman sometimes borrowed from William Faulkner and James Joyce, but he shaped and fashioned the stream-of-consciousness technique, the main modernist technique he borrowed from Faulkner and Joyce, for his own purposes. The ending of *Glance* is an example. Overall, the dependence on Eliot limits *Glance,* especially when one compares it to Wideman's other books. Nevertheless, *Glance* affords glimpses of the writer drawing on other writers to develop his own technique and take his art into new regions.

When he wrote *Hurry Home,* Wideman plunged himself into the most innovative and experimental modernist fantasy form that he had yet constructed. Writers such as Faulkner and Joyce still clearly influenced him, but he structured the fantasy form of *Home* for the special purpose of depicting the mind of a confused, uncertain black man trying to elude black reality. For parts of the book, Cecil lives in the midst of the black community and tries to escape what he sees as its harmful environment. The fantasy form is used to convey Cecil's evasiveness as he attempts to escape an inescapable fact, the fact that he is a black man living among black people. *Home* is further complicated by ambivalence toward Cecil and his attitudes in the narrative itself and by its own paradox, which shows both Cecil and the narrative to be at cross-purposes. The portrayal of Cecil's fantasy world insulated from black reality tested Wideman's creative skills and carried him into frontier regions beyond *Glance*. In its formal aspects *Home* sometimes bogs down in complication and opacity. It nevertheless contains much very impressive writing.

Lynchers is clearly the best written of Wideman's early books, but Wideman still does not articulate the full black voice in which he speaks in the Homewood trilogy. In part of *Lynchers'* structure, Wideman breaks the modernist fantasy mold and builds around dramatic, external events. In its riveting plot *Lynchers* differs from either *Glance* or *Home*. Fantasy and surrealism, on the other hand, project an intense black worldview forged in oppression. Wideman's command of black language had not been impressive before *Lynchers*, but in this book, he makes black language an important conveyor of the black ethos. In *Lynchers*, then, Wideman demonstrates progress toward achieving a black voice but not its full attainment.

In *Hiding Place*, Wideman finally brings together the mainstream modernist tradition and the black cultural tradition in such a way as to achieve a black voicing of problems common to the traditions. Much of the technique in *Hiding Place* is stream of consciousness. As in *Lynchers*, the technique conveys the black worldview. But Wideman's primary formal gain in the book is the depiction of the black language practices and rituals that transmit the values, customs, and attitudes of the rich black cultural tradition that allow *Hiding Place's* characters to overcome alienation, fear, and frustration. *Lynchers* is in many ways a tour de force of black language, but *Hiding Place* explores the broad resources and uses of black language to an even greater extent. With form, theme, and language in *Hiding Place* Wideman achieves a much stronger black voicing than he did in *Lynchers*.

The strengths of *Damballah* in many ways parallel those in *Hiding Place*, but the black voicing in *Damballah* is even fuller and stronger than it was in *Hiding Place*. The range of characters, rituals, and folk forms is greater, and the black voicing is also stronger because the focus is more uniformly on the black tradition and not initially on characters separated from the tradition in alienation, frustration, and fear, as in *Hiding Place*. Wideman shows great skill in portraying the black tradition in *Damballah*.

In *Sent for You Yesterday*, Wideman for the first time began to explore the postmodernist approach in his fiction; he began to strive for a black voicing of postmodernism that would give him the freedom to improvise and experiment, especially with regard to the black experience, that modernism did not afford. Wideman's treatment of the black experience using postmodernism in *Yesterday* is impressive. He achieved a black voicing of postmodernism from a black intellectual perspective that is distinct from the black folk perspective but still supportive of the black folk and black cultural tradition.

Reuben is a black voicing of postmodernism that indicates the depth and richness of black tradition, and its central intellectual figure supports that tradition. *Reuben's* postmodernist form requires Wideman to experiment with new devices because it encompasses the ideas of an unrestrained, fully realized intellectual who has a clearly articulated postmodernist view of the world. *Reuben* may be Wideman's most experimental and innovative book, but it reflects technical skill as well.

Hurry Home and *Lynchers* represent achievements of a different sort: they treat important themes in black literature. *Hiding Place*, *Damballah*, and *Yesterday*, which were written after a period of reading and discovery on Wideman's part, are noteworthy as they explore the rituals, beliefs, and attitudes in the black tradition. Cecil's attitude toward the black community in *Hurry Home* reveals a serious problem in black identity, one that Wideman shared, according to the evidence of his own biographical sketch. In its thematic focus the book is provocative and important because it analyzes the black psyche in the crucible of the Western intellectual tradition. *Home* is not, however, just a one-sided depiction of Cecil's views or of middle-class values, like some works written before and during the Harlem Renaissance. In presenting Wideman's and Cecil's ambivalence and identity crises it does not neglect their absurd and tragic aspects. *Home* highlights the genuine difficulty of Cecil's situation but does not try to hide the problems involved. (Two books that bear a general thematic similarity to *Home* and deal with educated, intelligent blacks are Nella Larsen's *Quicksand* and *Passing*.)

In *Lynchers*, Wideman moves from *Home*'s analysis of black avoidance of reality to an account of characters who must spend all their time trying, through revolutionary means, to reverse the devastating effects of centuries of black oppression. Only Richard Wright's *Native Son* comes to mind as a book of comparable effectiveness in its treatment of a destructive black experience and black frustration and ineffectuality in the face of white oppression. Wideman deals with a wider range of black life in *Lynchers,* however, than he does in *Home.*

After several years of preparing himself by reading other black writers and by moving closer to the family and community from which he had separated himself, Wideman unveiled a new literary approach in *Hiding Place* that placed him closer to other black writers dealing with the tensions between black tradition and the mainstream tradition. A primary difference between *Lynchers* and *Hiding Place* is the latter's emphasis on a black cultural tradition that can mitigate the effects of white oppression and provide wholeness and continuity for the black community; in other words, the main difference is the strong black voice in which Wideman speaks. *Hiding Place* is also noteworthy for its treatment of the mystical and magical in black tradition. Recently, such writers as Ishmael Reed and Toni Morrison have paid serious attention to the mystical and magical in black experience. Before they and Wideman did so, black writers had left this segment of the black tradition relatively unexplored. Wideman's redirection in his career therefore takes him into an area of the tradition that calls for investigation.

Wideman gives a very vivid fictional impression of a crucial side of black life and tradition in *Hiding Place.* In *Hiding Place,* there is magical contact with traditional values and ways through memory and dream, but traditional language rituals also guide the characters and produce phenomena for which there is no rational explanation (Bess's discovery of the number by the "numberology and trickology" ritual is an example). People also feel a mystical kind of unity in the community in *Hiding Place.* Family members feel it, and Clement senses it particularly in his relationship with Bess. These feelings, attitudes, and approaches to life are what one sees and hears talk about in black communities.

In *Damballah,* the Homewood saga and the triumphs and trials of Wideman's family revitalize the conventions of black tradition. In its first story, *Damballah* sets forth the idea that the black tradition is transmitted over time by its spirit or ghost, but *Damballah* largely emphasizes the more conventional in black tradition, particularly its Christian religious practices and beliefs. Although writers have paid more attention to this area of the tradition, Wideman's presentation is fresh and worthwhile.

Sent for You Yesterday projects as strong a view of the magical and mystical as *Hiding Place*. One thing *Yesterday* does is afford a glimpse of the voodoo and conjure practices that black people combine with their Christian beliefs (as Lizabeth's Aunt Aida and Uncle Bill do, for example). But more important, the whole black tradition is a magical, mystical spirit of music that is concentrated in certain individuals and transmitted from one generation to the next. In view of the prominent place that music occupies in black culture, one must say that Wideman may be expressing another legitimate view of the black tradition, although it may have a particularly intellectual slant in *Yesterday*.

The reshaping of Wideman's imagination and sensibility around black tradition and life brought impressive results. For Wideman to change, moreover, Wideman's efforts had to be nothing short of heroic. He covered a tremendous amount of ground between *Home* (and even *Lynchers*) and *Hiding Place*, and he thoroughly immersed himself in his task. Excellent books were the result. The achievement testifies to the seriousness of Wideman's commitment to being a writer.

After *Lynchers*, Wideman's first job was to study black folk culture thoroughly and to recreate aspects of it. When he had done so, he set out to bring his black intellectual characters, who were his main concern, and himself as an intellectual who shared ideas with his characters, into a meaningful, constructive relationship with folk culture and the black community. This integration of the intellectual into the community is, of course, related to Wideman's development of respect for the black tradition and his distancing of mainstream modernist tradition, which often involves the alienation of the intellectual from the community. Given the intellectual's estrangement in *Home*, and the intellectuals' collective failure to be effective in *Lynchers*, Wideman had to make their engagement with the community a slow, careful process. He started to develop the links in *Damballah* by relying heavily on characters who, like him, were writers and lived in Wyoming. In *Yesterday* he could make the return to the community complete by portraying an intellectual who was trying to find his way home very much as Wideman had done. The characters' close kinship to Wideman meant that it would be difficult for them to establish rapport; they had to overcome the same problems of alienation that Wideman the writer-intellectual knew from his experience to be extremely difficult. But like Wideman they had skill, seriousness, and tenacity, so that their attempt was successful, and their success was Wideman's too. By the time he wrote *Reuben*, Wideman was ready to depict an intellectual fully at home in his black environment and able to be his intellectual self at the same time.

Each of the three books also has a more specific thematic and ideological relevance as a way station on the intellectual's journey. *Damballah* documents his failure and his painful breakthrough to a tentative place in the community. The struggle of the intellectual in *Damballah*, especially in "Across the Wide Missouri," includes some of the most poignant moments in all of Wideman's writing. *Yesterday* examines the ways in which the intellectual's thinking differs from that of the folk and shows him developing the inner resources he needs to live among the folk. At the same time, it demonstrates both the need for him to compromise and his willingness to do so. *Reuben* gives the intellectual unfettered range, full metaphysical flight. But it also forces him to return from the lofty atmosphere to take into account the needs of the people who live in the streets. In many ways, it brings intellectual extremes back to daily life.

Between *Yesterday* and *Reuben*, Wideman published the biographical-autobiographical *Brothers and Keepers*; Brothers anchors Wideman in the community so that he can take off on even higher intellectual flights in *Reuben*. One might say that *Brothers* treats the intellectual's isolation from the people and his attempt to return to them, or at least the intellectual's effort to confront the implications of life among the people, in a more direct way than *Yesterday*. The reason is that *Brother* with its nonfictional form involves an even closer tie between its character John and Wideman than that between John and Wideman in *Damballah* or that between Doot and Wideman in *Yesterday*. *Brothers* sets Wideman's intellectual compromise and return to the black community on a personal, individual, concrete level not evident in *Damballah* and *Yesterday*. Its strength and honesty are great.

Wideman is exemplary in his consistent struggle to push his craft into new areas and to write excellent fiction. He is also exemplary in his quest to reshape his focus and change his intellectual direction in order to make his work more relevant to black people while he expresses his creative self. No contemporary writer has worked harder with greater results. Wideman, a man of vast talent, is one of the major writers to emerge during the last twenty-five years.

Appendix
Interview with John Edgar Wideman, 12 August 1988

COLEMAN: In a 1982 interview, you say that in *Damballah*, published along with *Hiding Place* in 1981, you did not want to exclude the segment of your audience familiar with T. S. Eliot, James Joyce, and William Faulkner, the audience toward which, I believe, your first two books, *A Glance Away* and *Hurry Home,* were largely focused. But you made it clear that you were changing your focus in *Damballah* and writing a book with a broader scope that would be relevant to a black audience. You have not presented any extensive public statements about your fiction since *Sent for You Yesterday,* your next book after *Damballah,* but I see another change in your fiction, beginning with *Sent for You Yesterday* and even more clearly manifesting itself in *Reuben.* The emphasis is still on black community and culture, but it seems to me that Doot in *Sent for You Yesterday* and the character Reuben in *Reuben* take these books in somewhat different directions from *Hiding Place* and *Damballah* and also from your earlier work. Would you comment on this?

WIDEMAN: I guess the best comment would be "whatever book I'm working on now," because what you are talking about I believe is that endless process of backward and forward and overlap and self-echoing and recapitulation that is a career, that is an evolution of a way of seeing, eventually of a vision. I think in my own mind there is a sharp break, in some ways, between the first three books and the next two or three; but that's only sharp because I became conscious of it, I think, and began to talk about the break myself—that is, the movement towards other kinds of audience and the conscious attempt to include the audience members of my family represent. But even in the first three books, as I look back on them now, I was very much concerned with family and community and the people I grew up with, and I thought, in my own way, that I was addressing that audience quite directly. But then, on rereading the work and rethinking it—those earlier works—it seemed to me that I was missing the boat in some ways, that I had not done as well as I might possibly be able in inviting that audience, and I had done some things that probably worked against including that audience. But that was in retrospect. In all honesty, as I look back on the first three books, I was writing about who I was and what had happened to me and people that I knew, things that were important, but then I grew, and my sense of who I was and what constituted the important events in my past changed, and I hope it continues to change, and so the process is evolutionary, it's moving; and as writer, as artist, I'm like everybody else who experiences the books, both inside and outside, and so there is a process of the actual evolution of the work and then there is also my awareness of what's going on in the work, and my ability to stop it, change it, or give it direction, or to focus it. And so those are two things that are happening. A good critic, a certain kind of reader, may have more success, or may at an earlier stage figure out these changes, anticipate ways the work should go, ways that the work isn't going. So that's a long way of making the first distinction, that often—well, it has to come after the fact. There was no game plan at the beginning which was scuttled for another game plan somewhere in the middle. There is always back and forward and testing. I think the character of the crippled woman in my very first book, the grandmother . . .

COLEMAN: Martha?

WIDEMAN: Yes, that is for me, in many ways, as much a picture of my grandmother as the one that occurs in *Sent for You Yesterday.*

COLEMAN: The thing about *A Glance Away,* particularly, is that many of the characters and many of the incidents are very similar, I would venture to say the same, to those we find in later books, that is, in *Hiding Place* and *Damballah* and other books. So it is obvious that you have been dealing with, it seems to me, the same family and very similar materials. What I see as a critic is how your approach has changed in the later books. It seems to me that you treat the materials somewhat differently in the books, particularly beginning with *Hiding Place* and *Damballah*. So there is a lot of consistency there as well as difference.

WIDEMAN: It's kind of funny to look back, because I don't always maintain a very clear picture in my own head of the other books . . . in fact . . . in the sense that they all sort of blend together, and once a book is finished I never go back and read it again. So if you are writing a critique of my work you probably would be much more adept at calling out the names of characters and whatnot than I would be.

COLEMAN: You never read a book again?

WIDEMAN: I have never read a book straight through after it's been published, because then it's out of my hands. I have read parts of some and I go through them maybe if I'm going to give a reading or if I am going to give an interview or something like that. I might review it just for informational purposes, but it's the writing that's important. It's the writing that engages me. So once the book is finished, there is no more. . . . it's not live any more. I can't do anything else with it. Also it's a little intimidating, maybe negatively intimidating. If there's something. . . , if I don't like the book, that would be a problem because there it is—it's out there. Plus it's also just being finished with something, really finished with it. You start with some small idea, and it grows, and you work on it for a couple of years and then it becomes a book and then it goes through the publication process, which means reading drafts and reading version after version, having it copy edited and you're just tired of it by that time. Maybe there will be a point in my life where I will want to go back and look at some of these things, but at this point it doesn't seem likely—I think I'd rather continue to move ahead.

COLEMAN: So critics and creative writers in a lot of ways have different perspectives or maybe different jobs, different tasks, would you say? Because critics, people like me, are trying to make sense of things and we just hope that we don't impose too much on the writer, although I guess you can't help doing that, can you?

WIDEMAN: Well, you have an agenda, everybody has an agenda, and everybody has a . . . critics particularly have sometimes hidden, sometimes very exclusive motives for looking at any kind of literature, whether it's to get tenure, or to prove that whites are superior to blacks, or to prove that one culture is dominant to another, or to prove that one writer deserves all the goodies and others should just shut up. . . , or to prove that you are smarter than anybody else, that you know more about this. There are just as many reasons for writing a critical book as there are for writing a novel, maybe more. Because for a critical book you use your front brain a little more, so you are thinking, and often a book of fiction or poems is written with the back brain, so you haven't really thought out why you are doing it; the motivation is unconscious. So in that sense there may be more reasons for writing a critical book.

COLEMAN: Let me move on to another area here slightly different. You also said in this same interview that I just alluded to, that between the publication of *The Lynchers* in '73 and *Hiding Place* and *Damballah* in '81, you were learning a different fictional voice and a different language to talk about the experience in your fiction. Now, it is my perception that your fictional voice grows and matures over time. That is one thing I try to talk about as a critic. How does the voice. . . , how would you say the voice in *Hiding Place* and *Damballah* differs from the voice in *A Glance Away* and *Hurry Home,* the books before *Hiding Place?*

WIDEMAN: One way they differ is simple enough, and that is I get older, and as I get older, maybe I become exposed to more. And I think also I grow. . . . I hope I am growing more independent. I hope I have stopped saying what I think people might want me to say and have gotten more confident about saying what I want to say, and in my own fashion. I think that's why old men can wear frazzled-collar shirts and young men wouldn't be caught dead in them, you know, because you're just paying too much attention to your audience when you're younger—in a bad way. So that's part of it—just a simple process of maturation.

COLEMAN: You think you were paying . . . in the earlier books in what sense were you paying attention to audience?

WIDEMAN: What sense?

COLEMAN: Or to what audience?

WIDEMAN: For me audience was something that I took for granted. My sense of audience came from my education up to that point, my sense of what the important works of Western literature were, my sense of the classics, my sense of the esthetics that govern those classics; and so I saw myself as writing for that tradition. The notion of a separate audience and the notion of another set of obligations that I might have as a writer, was very faint indeed. I thought that, yes, I would be bringing my own personal experience, therefore, a black experience, into this world of letters, but I didn't see myself as necessarily changing that world. So, I guess an analogy would be something like the early notions of integration. You go to the lunch counter and that's enough. Just so you get in and you're served there. And then later politically people figured out that that certainly wasn't enough, that the problem wasn't the lunch counter at all; the problem was the whole system that buttressed that kind of segregation. So that going to the lunch counter was an important first step, but then to really obtain some kind of freedom and some sort of autonomy and independence, it was necessary to penetrate the system—in a way deconstruct the system—and begin to own lunch counters, and begin to even say that the lunch counters are jive anyway, and that maybe what you want is to eat in a totally different place, and different food, and a different hour, et cetera, et cetera. I think in my writing I reflect some of this. As I look back it seems to me that I was too easily seduced into believing there was only one way to do things and that my job as a writer was to learn how to do things that way and be accepted because I had learned to jump through the hoops in the proper way.

COLEMAN: And a lot of that is along the tradition of the great—so-called—great white writers, i.e., Joyce, Faulkner, Eliot, people like that, that tradition?

WIDEMAN: Exactly. The people who were on graduate exams thirty years ago, and still are, but there are distinctions that need to be made, because I still think those writers are powerful writers. I still use their models in some situations. The problem is to identify what I do and the changes that I have gone through along cultural lines rather than racial lines. Look at a writer like William Faulkner; he is saturated by elements of black southern culture. And so to say that what I needed to do was get rid of "white influences" doesn't really portray, doesn't really accurately reflect, what was going on. What I had to do was . . . what I think I have been able to do is look at these influences in terms other than race, so that I still am responsive to Faulkner's attempts to capture the oral cadences of southern speech—and often southern black speech—in those long flowing sentences, in that kind of crazy mix of vocabularies which comes from the King James Bible and from proverbs and illiteracies and all the rest. I still respect that. Joyce's improvisa-tions and spontaneity, inventiveness with language are very, very important, still part and parcel of what I am doing. But I am doing it and using those models both because they are powerful examples and because I am responding to them, responding to techniques, to power in them that reflects my own cultural experience. I can draw from them in the way that, let's say, black religion drew from traditional African religions, the way that traditional African religious beliefs could find in Christian churches' familiar practices, concepts, eventually a home—things from baptism to all the other parallels. So I don't want to make it seem that I exchanged one set of masters for another, because I hope that what I am doing is internalizing many different influences and shuffling among those and picking and choosing. And that's the key. Early on, not having the sophistication and knowledge to be able to pick and choose, because I was only familiar with one tradition. And then there is one more trick—and this is a very long answer, I know, but there is one more trick—the black influences were never *not* there. Nobody had ever pointed out to me how they were there. A Faulkner and a Joyce are part of a world culture, and they have learned from Africa, they have learned things from the street, they have learned things from the process of urbanization. In other words, we share a common culture and it wasn't made clear to me, as I grew up and I was educated, that Faulkner was, for instance, dependent on black culture for many of the virtues of his writing.

COLEMAN: One thing I try to point out, one thing that I see in what I call the maturing of your voice, and this is what I was trying to get at earlier, is that you bring together these various influences from white writers, from black writers, but also from black people in general, from the oral tradition, from black ritual, and so forth. And particularly in the books after *The Lynchers*, starting with *Hiding Place*, that's what makes your literary voice there deep and mature, for me. So it's not so much that there really are new things there. As you said, the black influences were there from the beginning, and they are still there, but to me there is a different kind of blend, and there is a different kind of emphasis. And it seems to me it's that emphasis that creates the maturity in your voice. It seems to me that you draw on black resources much better, much more fully, than you did in the earlier works.

WIDEMAN: Well, I hope so, and part of that is very conscious, because I went to school to those voices. They were always part of me, but I made an attempt to—by reading other black writers, by reading slave narratives, by immersing myself for a number of years in as many different aspects of black culture as I could, as was reasonable—I tried to learn and bring to my fingertips so it was second nature, but also have in my mind, exactly what those cultural resources were. So I studied them. I made that a study, the same way I had made *Ulysses* a study, the same way I studied Eliot: read about Eliot, learned where he grew up, read critics, analyzed his poems, wrote papers. I did the same thing for Afro-American culture, and I think that gave me much more access, and I could consciously use it. I had used black culture before in *The Lynchers*. I had also used black history before in a whole slew of incidents that began *The Lynchers*, and I was just at that time beginning to understand where those kinds of techniques were coming from, and why they might seem appropriate; but then in the later books also I began to understand how in using Afro-American folklore and language I didn't have to give up any of the goals that I was after when I was using more Europeanized and more traditional—literary traditional—devices and techniques. I didn't have to give up a thing. I could talk about the most complicated and sophisticated and intense moments and understandings and characters in the Afro-American idiom. That was a real breakthrough, but it was a breakthrough that didn't come accidentally. It was a result of study and concentration, and research in fact.

COLEMAN: In the book *Reuben*, the character there, it seems to me, is a servant of the black community. Reuben is very conscious of helping people in the black community, although on certain levels Reuben is a spirit—as I think you called him in some little thing I read about the book once—but it seems to me that in a lot of ways he is also a real person as well as being a spirit—if that is true—who is a servant of the black community. But Reuben says explicitly—and I think I see a connection here with Doot in *Sent for You Yesterday,* although it's not explicit in *Sent for You Yesterday.* But Reuben is always talking about creating fictions, fictions that will create positive illusions in the black community, as well as fictions that will undo, undercut, will subvert negative fictions perpetuated by the white community. Now, this is your first book at least where that kind of language has been explicit, certainly. Can you talk about that a little bit? What about Reuben as a servant of the community who lives in this nebulous world where he uses fictions and also deconstructs fictions and, it seems to me, that at some points in that book the narrative even deconstructs, briefly. Can you talk some about that—what's going on there? And it does seem to me that this has a lot to do with what I see as a development in your fiction, too.

WIDEMAN: Well, it's one thing to be able to pick out items of folklore, items of black culture, and use them in a particular fiction. That's one process, but I think that process becomes much more powerful and deeper when one has an understanding of the meaning of those rituals and those items, that is, try to restore them to the integrity in which they exist within the culture. Call and response is not just a coincidence. It is an attempt by a community to come to some set of values, to work out right and wrong, to build themselves into a cohesive unit by this kind of, in one way, political device which is working out together what things mean, what is being said. Call and response. Okay, so that fits into the deep structure of culture, and I have been lucky because I've been able to . . . I have had the time to think about how these items of folklore fit into the larger picture and have begun to be able to capture—try to capture—some of their meaning within the fiction; so that I am writing—I would hope—from the inside out, rather than applying a sort of local color or pieces of exotica to a fiction which is related to those items only very tangentially. And that's my way of saying that Reuben has no choice but to be a servant of the people. He manifests a certain principle of magic. He manifests a principle of word magic that enables us to create our own institutions, our own identities, and he is a figure who will always be in the midst of trouble because the dominant culture resists any attempt to infringe on its power. And Reuben is a power figure. He is an intermediary. He is in the battleground. It's his job to untangle people from the negative effects of the dominant culture, to protect people from one another and also from these invidious forces that are all around them. That's a ritualistic process. It is the same thing that a shaman or a priest does on a traditional culture, and so he is a lawyer. But both plots and themes of the fictions I write, and the fictions themselves, are an attempt to subvert one notion of reality with others, to show that there is not simply one way of seeing things but many ways of seeing things. And as a people and as individuals if we don't jump into the breach, if we don't fight the battle of defining reality in our own terms, then somebody else will always come along and do it for us. So that *The Lynchers* is another way of looking at the 60's. The book *Reuben* is another way of looking at what's happened after the so-called civil rights revolution, et cetera. And Reuben himself, the character within the novel, is engaged in a struggle that I think I'm engaged in as writer outside the novel, creating and sustaining a version of reality to compete with those destructive versions which are tearing us apart.

COLEMAN: Is there a particular point or time when you become conscious of doing this in your writing, precisely what you talked about there?

WIDEMAN: Well, delusions of grandeur probably start pretty early, but specifically it began very clearly in a kind of nascent form in *Hurry Home*, and that's a book about cultural conflict. That's a book about somebody torn between two worlds, Mallarmé and the Faun, that imagery—somebody's part human, part something else—and the book is full of splits and double personalities and that kind of stress that comes there, but I think I had not learned to, in a sense, lexify that struggle in indigenous Afro-American terms. I was still reaching to other places for metaphors and symbols, and they are still valid to a certain extent, but they don't have that local force and particularity that are most appropriate for me in my works. So I had to shop around quite a bit more. *The Lynchers* is an important book in this sense, because I knew clearly in that book that something was wrong . . . , something . . . , and I saw more in political and sociological . . . .

COLEMAN: Something was wrong with what you were saying?

WIDEMAN: No, something was . . . the struggle for a kind of peace or a kind of independence . . . got hotter and hotter. It wasn't a literary concept, but it became a very personal concept. I felt threatened. I felt very threatened, and the threat to me was not only personal, it was a threat to a whole people. I saw as lots of us did, paranoid versions of— well, not so paranoid—versions of a country that was just going to self-destruct because of its racism, and a country which was at kind of a crossroads and had to make some really basic choices. Was it going to move a little bit to accommodate new voices—young peoples' voices, black peoples' voices, voices of change—or was it going to puff up its chest and send out the immigrants to whip on the black people again. And I felt that threat very personally and tried to talk about it in *The Lynchers*, but I still didn't have the vocabulary, I still didn't have the tools I required. I wasn't quite ready to set up a totally independent ground of reckoning. I didn't have the words yet. I didn't have the words yet to make the stand that I wanted to make. So the novel *The Lynchers* is about things coming apart, things destructing. Then the next books are an attempt to reconstruct what came apart.

COLEMAN: It seems to me that in *The Lynchers*—and I distinctly remember reading that; I must have read it in about '74, so not too long after it came out—and it was, and still is, an extremely powerful book. One thing that is very powerful about it is the language. There is a sense there that you know so much about black culture, black ritual, black language, much more a sense that you know about that than in the first two books. Now, of course, you did, but it comes out so much more in *The Lynchers*. The thing about *The Lynchers* though, as you say, is that things are so torn apart for black people, things are so hopeless, in a sense, and it is not until you get to *Hiding Place* and the books after that—*Hiding Place* and *Damballah*, particularly—where I find you bringing together what you have in *The Lynchers* with other aspects of black life, black culture, that create a kind of wholeness, a kind of broad perspective. Now it's not sentimentalized or anything, what I am talking about in *Hiding Place*, but it's there—what I'm calling wholeness at this point, at least.

WIDEMAN: It's clear to me—at least for the moment as we sit here and talk—that there is in *The Lynchers* . . . thematically it's very similar to *Reuben* and the later books, because it's all about the attempt of a group of black men to substitute, by use of myth and by use of a kind of a play—a kind of a strange passion play, a lynching—to break through the hold of one illusion of reality into a new day where there might be some room for change, and that's what the book is about, about constructive change. But it's a very negative myth and it's a myth that still . . . it's a borrowed myth, the myth of the lynching, or the ritual of the lynching. So it's borrowed from the oppressor. And it's negative. What happens in the later books I think is—if we want to simplify it, I guess—the attempt to find positive rituals and myths that can shore up, that can reconstruct, the sense of reality in the black community, in its own terms, in terms that have been there all along, so there is that kind of distinction, I think. Now, where you put the book *Reuben* in all of this is another question, because *Reuben* has a lot of the pessimism of *The Lynchers*, but Reuben still goes at it from a positive point of view, as a traditional healer and magician.

COLEMAN: One thing is very clear in *Reuben*, and what pointed me to this was the acknowledgment of Robert Farris Thompson's book *Flash of the Spirit*, which I got and read. Part of what Reuben is using there, probably consciously, is aspects of Kongo cosmology and myth as part of his structure. Now, that's something that is a little bit, or maybe more than a little bit, different in your work, isn't it? I mean the specific use of African . . . well, maybe not—I'm about to say something that isn't true—because African and of course Afro-American are close and at a lot of points not separable, but still it seems to me that *Reuben* is, at least on a conscious level, doing something that your other characters haven't done, in terms of drawing on African motifs and myths.

WIDEMAN: Again the process of self-education of the author and the ability to get some of that, some of what I learned, into the books, I think that's the simple way of explaining it or at least describing it. Explaining it is more complicated. It seems to me that what I am after, and what I would like to achieve, is not just the external changes that might enable a black guy or a black woman to walk into this two-hundred-thousand-dollar-a-year job in IBM, but to have that person—that black man or that black woman—earn a very good living and change IBM's act somehow. Or if that black man or that black woman had a chance to go into IBM, to make that person an agent for change, to make that person conscious of what's wrong with that step up as well as what the benefits are. To be able to critique it, to have choices, and to that extent, I'm working from the ground up. I want . . . the books have to reflect the deeper spiritual values that animate, for me, what's good and what should be preserved about Afro-American life. The rituals are a manifestation of some spirit force, which runs much deeper. That's why the outward shape or description of the culture can change. But it can maintain its integrity because of those forces that run underground. Those forces have always been there. And those are the ones I'm trying to touch upon. I might do something like try to show how Kongo cosmology might be relevant to what Reuben's doing—how it's tied up—the notion of doubles, the notion of two worlds. I want to show how that is as relevant as looking at the American. You can understand the American experience or the Afro-American experience in Kongo terms as well as in terms of Calvinism and Protestantism and Roman Catholicism and Western humanism. Those are ways, those are containers—jails for the culture—which don't explain everything that needs to be explained, so I'm looking for other explanations.

COLEMAN: It seems to me that Doot in *Sent for You Yesterday* is creating a kind of myth or a story of Afro-American culture with black music and black musicians as symbols. I see that as one thing that's different about *Sent for You Yesterday*. The music and the musicians are certainly very important in *Hiding Place* and *Damballah* and also in the earlier books, too. But it appears to me that Doot is doing something—as an individual—is doing something different there. What is Doot doing in *Sent for You Yesterday?* And of course it's very complex because at points Doot is clearly the first-person narrator, I mean, he is the "I" narrator who is right there in the narrative. At points he seems to merge with an omniscient narrator, but it seems to me that he is deeply embedded in the whole structure. What's he doing?

WIDEMAN: Well, he's learning to dance, and he's learning to dance to music that is not totally explicable in natural terms. That is, the music

is magical. The music has a force that can't be explained in any
satisfactory everyday way. The music seems to have an energy all its
own that is rooted some place other than in individuals. And so in that
sense the music is the pulse, the rhythm, the force, the expression of
the entire culture; and by learning to dance Doot is learning to, like a
fish, live in this medium.

COLEMAN: Music almost says something that language, that words, can't
say?

WIDEMAN: Well, it subsumes them, or language aspires to the condition of
music. Music seems to me the medium that comprehends all others,
because music can be silent. It can be Magic playing basketball,
without a sound track, just his movements. Or it can be a woman
dancing or it can be just somebody walking down the street . . . , so
when you see people playing basketball, that music is there, even
though it's not audible. It's the rhythm of the walk, it's the rhythm of
the movement. So music seems to be just a medium of expression that
subsumes the other. But where Doot comes into all this, he's a
protagonist, and he's learning to dance in this medium, so that makes
him the perfect exemplar of the writer. Because the book is about
creating a useful past, creating a past that will sustain an identity and
open doors towards the future, for the writer as well as the character. So
the book is enacting in its composition that experience of letting the
culture energize it and carry it along; in other words, the words are
learning to dance, the words are learning to depend on their roots and
their sources in Afro-American tradition. So that's what was happening
to me as author. I was letting go, I was relaxing into that medium and
that's what Doot is doing also, as a character within the story. And so
there is naturally a great exchange between that Doot inside and the
author outside, because they are all working toward dancing to the
same music.

COLEMAN: Another thing that I'm very much interested in is the way that
your main, primary characters who are academically trained, who are
intellectuals, try to find their place in the black community in *Damballah* in particular. In several of the pieces here I see that process of
the writer—and it sometimes is obviously, clearly a writer—that process of the writer-intellectual trying to find his voice, his place. "The
Chinaman" is a good example of that. "The Watermelon Story," I think,
is a good example, although it is a very perplexing story in a lot of
ways. "Across the Wide Missouri" is another example and I think in
some ways "The Beginning of Homewood" really brings the theme of
the quest of the writer-intellectual together in a lot of ways—not that it
necessarily reaches closure, but it does reach a kind of finish, at least
for this particular volume. Would you talk about that process of what
the writer and intellectual is doing there in terms of finding his voice or
his place in a black community and tradition?

WIDEMAN: The novelist or the writer is a storyteller, and the process for me that is going to knit up the culture, knit up the fabric of the family, the collective family—all of us—one crucial part of that process is that we tell our own stories. That we learn to tell them and we tell them in our own words and that they embrace our values and that we keep on saying them, in spite of the madness, the chaos around us, and in spite of the pressure not to tell it. And so that storytelling activity is crucial to survival, individual survival, community survival. So the storyteller, the artist, is a crucial member of the community. He is also someone who perhaps by definition is outside the community—and should be and will always be—and so that yearning to be part of it may be one of the natural conditions of being a storyteller. Storytellers are always inside and outside the story by definition. Sometimes in Afro-American culture there are these little doors, there are these wonderful windows by which the storyteller gets pulled back, so he doesn't feel too lonely, doesn't feel left out. The call-and-response business, everybody sitting around on a mat sharing a story, the redaction of older stories, the retelling them. So our tradition seems to have a way that, yes, you can come back home again. If you tell your stories in a certain fashion, we'll help you tell them, they'll be ours, we'll reclaim them. And so I think my writer figure is the taleteller who is in that inevitably divided position. He has a voice, he's using it in a constructive way, but he also wants to blend, to merge. That voice to achieve its fullest resonance needs the voices of the rest of the community. And so, in all the stories that theme and that figure occur. The writer off, thrusting himself above the action to check it out and then trying to reengage, trying to be part of the very story he's telling.

COLEMAN: The process of reengagement is very clear throughout *Damballah*, as I said, but particularly in that last piece, "The Beginning of Homewood," where the writer draws upon the voices of community and family people, particularly Aunt May, to tell the story, but finally by the end he still has to rely on his own voice, which has incorporated or perhaps subsumed those other voices. It seems to me that in later books, particularly *Reuben*, for example, you have a figure who is set above and away from the community in a lot of ways, but is also a very fundamental part of the community. So, I guess that tension remains, that whole process of moving toward reengagement and I suppose moving away, but the distance, or some distance, is probably always there.

WIDEMAN: Yes, and it's not always pleasant, but it's the condition for creativity. The wound comes first and then the healing and then the growth.

COLEMAN: Wally in *Reuben* is an educated character. He is different from Reuben, in a sense, but he has got the University of Pennsylvania background, the formal education. In fact he has a formal education that Reuben does not have, but the more important point is that he seems to represent the destructive, and Reuben seems to represent the constructive. Is this true? What does Wally represent for you?

WIDEMAN: Wally is out there. He has been kicked in the behind an awful lot and the worst kinds of kicks, because often they were disguised as bones. You know, he bent over to get the bone and found a foot in his ass, and that happened to him a lot. And even the bones he picks up and chews on he finds out very often they have been laced with arsenic or that they are not bones at all, that they are fake; they are pieces of wood or pieces of stone. So that's been the kind of experience he's had. It doesn't necessarily make a very pleasant personality, and so he is out there in a sense of, "Well, I get done in, and somebody seems to be making a living off doing me in so I'll return the favor in kind. It's war. I'm out here all on my own and I'll do the best I can and not look back." That's his attitude, and it's a very common attitude. In an educated person it shocks the at-large society more because they say, look, he had all the advantages, he had all those privileges, he could be an honorary white guy if he only played his cards right. And also, he's a dangerous and threatening person because he did get some of the goodies. He did follow . . . he looked at the carrot and followed it, and so the notion that you can control a subject people by letting a few of them off the hook becomes threatened by Wally, because he is one of your honorary white men and he's turned against you. So I think for me Wally embodies a lot of that, that kind of stuff—the rage, the anger that is inchoate but is always possibly there to burst out. And for me, a guy like Wally, what he doesn't do or does do is less important than that edge, that violent edge that he's forced to live on. Because that's destructive of his personal integrity; whether or not he strikes out and hurts someone else, he is already a victim, he has already lost. But he's not totally lost, because he's tough and he does have a friend that he cares about, he cares about this Reuben, and he's smart enough to know that he's missing something. He's smart enough to know that, if he lets himself become a kind of an educated Bigger Thomas, that he's sort of cooperating in the final act of his own destruction, and so there is part of him that is resisting that. He doesn't want to give his enemy that satisfaction. Those are some things I think about him. Reuben sees possibility in him; in fact, Reuben likes him, has a kind of affection for him, and in fact he turns to Wally when he's in trouble.

COLEMAN: And Wally does come to his assistance. This relates, I think, to something that I was talking about earlier and maybe the answer to this is obvious. I'm not sure. The writers in *Hiding Place* and *Damballah*, the characters who are writers, and there's a number in *Damballah*, often have your first name, John, and are part of a fictional family that is, I think, derived from your own family. Is there a particular significance to that, or is the answer to that obvious?

WIDEMAN: Well, it's a kind of a personal game that I play—sometimes. I use actual names of people, but they are not based on people who hold those names. And I thought it's kind of fun for people to see their names in print. And also, you know we've had a lot of problems with names in this country and being noticed as people, as individuals, and being on the record, and being part of history, being part of what counts. And so John French's name now is out there. He's on the record. Sometimes John French is like my grandfather, sometimes not like my grandfather, but either way he's on the record, and Harry Wideman is on the record. I'm on the record. But anybody who would try to make one-to-one correspondences, or think that the stories reflect the biographies of the people who hold the names would just get in a mire, and that's also kind of delightful to me. Because it's like a minefield, it's like a trap, because the further you go to try to connect the names to actual people, the more confusing it will be. Eventually you just come right back in a circle. But you see the family—my intimate, my personal family—could look at the names and play games and could identify to a certain degree. So there is a kind of a key, but even the key is not consistent. That is, they will see in Aunt May some things about the actual Aunt May. But then in the next paragraph there will be something that is really about Aunt Rachel, or Becky, or somebody else. So somebody in the family can have fun with it, because they can say, "Oh yeah, I remember when May did that," but the whole character is not May.

COLEMAN: So you have to be careful in going too far and making too much out of one-to-one correspondences.

WIDEMAN: Right. Even among books. You know I never sat down, for instance, and tried to figure out if Brother Small and Brother Tate, if I really wanted them to be the same person—you know, if the dates worked out and every other thing worked out—yes and no. It's a kind of shifting spirit . . ., so you couldn't take these books and find an orderly scheme of relationships and dates and time and correspondences, I don't think. I'm sure you couldn't.

COLEMAN: It seems to me that there is similarity and consistency, but if you try to structure it too tightly, then it will get out of hand. You really can't do that.

WIDEMAN: Well, they are stories, and as the Igbos say, all stories are true. And my own sense of identity, or the sense of identity which I am evolving as I write books, has a lot to do with the . . . what is fragmentary, what is discontinuous, more and more so. So that my whole way of looking at human beings and lives is changing all the time. I probably believe that more than most people that the notion of a stable, underpinning personality is itself a fiction. That people have different stages and go through different personas and they are really drastically, drastically different in the sense that you could talk about one person's life as many lives.

COLEMAN: In *Reuben* your setting is still Homewood, but you mention only a few of the Homewood characters you dealt with in previous books. Are you getting ready to move away from the Homewood material to deal with different material?

WIDEMAN: Well, the next book is about Philadelphia, but you can get the boy out of the country, but you can't get the country out of the boy. No matter what I write about it will be through the eyes of someone who grew up in a place like Homewood, and so there will always be connections.

COLEMAN: You once said that improvisation, what you called "writing on the edge," was very important to you. It seems to me that you have taken this kind of writing to new heights in *Reuben*. Would you say that's true?

WIDEMAN: I don't think that you can write a very meaningful book about a culture that's in flux, a culture that is changing all the time, and a culture which is infused with minority points of view which haven't been fully represented before—you can't write about a culture meaningfully and use the conventions and traditions of narrative fiction which have existed and grew out of attempts to describe that culture in other times and places. So that the connection between form and meaning is organic and in a book like *Reuben* if I want to tell the truth I have to invent ways of capturing. . . . I have to invent new nets for it, the old nets don't work. And so each book has to be an adventure in that sense. Each book is a redefinition of what counts and how it counts and how you can capture it.

COLEMAN: How would you describe the development of formal, stylistic qualities in your writing during your career? Is there a development there that you can talk about? You know critics, like me, always want to talk about development.

WIDEMAN: I like to take chances, and one chance that I have been taking lately, and continue to take, is a chance with the texture of the narrative—letters, hymns, poems, song lyrics, thoughts, speech, time present, time past, future time, philosophic discourse, scatting, etc., etc. . . . a kind of collage . . . you find in somebody like an Eliot, but that you also find in traditional African art. In masks or dance, you have that eclectic combination. So that's one thing, that's one way I take chances. Another way is I try to invite the reader into the process of writing, into the mysteries, into the intricacies of how things are made and so, therefore, I foreground the self-consciousness of the act of writing. And try to get the reader to experience that, so that the reader is participating in the creation of the fiction. In fact I demand that and in fact scare lots of readers away, because that's not light stuff. But for me that's a funny version of call and response, my particular version of a communal work being made.

COLEMAN: Part of what you try to do in *Brothers and Keepers* is help your brother, Robby, but the book is also about your attempt to face yourself, your own life. Is that true?

WIDEMAN: Well, the book had a very instrumental purpose. It was to help Robby, help him legally, help him spiritually; but at the same time it was an attempt to help myself, because I was in a state of great despair because of his situation. I . . . felt helpless and needed to try to do something about it. I also learned that a lot of space and a lot of time had come between my brother and myself, and I didn't know who he was. And of course I felt somewhat guilty about that and I thought well, hell, was there some way I might have been able to help, was there something I could have done to prevent this. Now, I still don't know the answers, but I do know now that everybody has their own life. You do the best you can. But the point of the book and the point of trying to rediscover who my brother was and have a relationship with him, all that reflected things that were going on, that were less personal. Questions I was sorting out, okay? I had separated myself in lots of ways from my family, because of my job, because of what I do. I had separated myself in lots of ways, physically and emotionally, from the larger black community, the majority of black people. And here was a situation in which my own brother was beckoning me, demanding that I pay attention, that I make some sense of that enormous gap between us. And so the book was an occasion for me to try to make sense of that, the enormous gap between myself and the place where I was born, the place where I grew up.

COLEMAN: Family, community . . .

WIDEMAN: Family, community . . . I was still in touch in many ways with family and community. Important, sustaining, natural ways. Yet I had lost touch also. I don't know exactly how to say it. I tried to say it in my book, but . . . There is a whole issue of what happens when anybody, any black person in this country, gains a skill, gains an education, gains some sort of power; whether it's a doctor, lawyer, businessman. How does that individual success relate to the fact that most people are far from successful in those economic terms, and how does success perpetuate the system that is in fact oppressing so many black people? And that issue is a vexed one and needs to be looked at and so *Brothers and Keepers* is an attempt to look at that as well. Systemically what does it mean that there can be one or two of us who are allowed to filter into professions, become college teachers, become writers? What is our responsibility, to ourselves, to the ones we left behind? Do we have to leave them behind? Are there ways that we can be successful without perpetuating the class and the racial hierarchy that produced this?

COLEMAN: Do you have any other comments about your work?

WIDEMAN: The trouble with talking about my work is that I become more and more self-conscious. What's involved is a process of simultaneous self-translation. A double-voiced voice. Writing is a unique act, a unique kind of process, and talk about it doesn't necessarily capture what the process is. In fact it distorts, and as much is lost as is gained. I hear what's being lost even as I speak. It's like digging myself deeper and deeper into a hole.

COLEMAN: I'm glad you're saying that because to some extent that lets critics off the hook. No, I'm joking; not really.

WIDEMAN: Talking about one's work can be an interesting activity and maybe some might even say it's necessary. I certainly know that readers are interested in deciphering the magic, but in fact it's the magic that draws them. That is, you can put together all the information possible about a writer or about a book and it still won't equal the book. And the writer can talk about it forever, and it won't produce a book, nor will he or she get close to reproducing the effects that the book produced in me, in the reader. So it's almost a kind of futile effort. And then there's my personal distaste for too much talk about what I'm writing. I believe it's dangerous to think of oneself as having a career, to allow oneself to become the object of prurient or even well-intentioned curiosity. Writers shouldn't be commodities. At best, talking about one's work is a strange, uncomfortable position to be in. To trot out one's interviewing head and interviewing face becomes a kind of comic process. There is a certain level at which I am constantly suppressing laughter. Anyway, why should we try to talk art into being any less of a mystery.

COLEMAN: What good are critics?

WIDEMAN: The good ones are very good. Criticism in this country, since it's such an established institution, reflects some of the worst things about the country. It tends toward *People Magazine* profiling, and it promotes an interest in the artist rather than an interest in the work. The work, if it's good, is doing serious business. Artists in their private lives often do pretty junky, tacky, trifling business. What I do or who I do it to and how I do it—these personal matters are just gossip. There's often a confusion between the person I am and what I do in my work. If the work is serious it should stand on its own. It shouldn't need the prop of a personality behind it. Another side of this cult of personality is that it perpetuates our confusion about race. The author's race or sex determines the kind of critical commentary that appears about his or her work. This stupidity is institutionalized in traditional literary studies. If we didn't have pictures of writers, would critics discuss books on the basis of what's in them? Furthermore, there is a tie between criticism and the academy that is somewhat unhealthy or very unhealthy at times. Academic critics sponsor reputations and the more information there is, then the more attractive you are to a certain kind of unimaginative, fact-collecting critic. Then more begets more. Gossip mongering, personality contests trivilialize art, and it will inevitably go that way if critics pander to the publishing industry's tendency to promote superstars and ignore art. . . . One reason I am sitting and talking with you the way I am is because writing by Afro-Americans remains a stepchild, and Afro-American critics, if given a chance, may be able to do things that their fellow critics don't do. Maybe the stake that you have in literature might be a little different, and if given a chance, you may be able to express what it is. There is at least one service you can perform. You can be a link between Afro-American writing and an Afro-American readership. That's my kind of not-so-hidden agenda when I give interviews like this. Ideally, the good critics will get the writer to audiences that are looking for him or waiting for him and his work.

COLEMAN: Thank you.

References

Barksdale, Richard, and Kinnamon, Keneth, eds. 1972. *Black Writers of America: A Comprehensive Anthology*. New York: Macmillan.

Bradbury, Malcolm, and McFarlane, James, eds. 1976. *Modernism: 1890–1930*. New York: Penguin.

Davis, Tonya Bolden. 1988. "Word Star." *Essence*, March, p. 26.

Eliot, T. S. *The Waste Land and Other Poems*. New York: Harcourt, 1934.

Frazier, Kermit. 1975. "The Novels of John Wideman." *Black World* 24:18–35.

Gates, Henry Louis, Jr., and Davis, Charles T., eds. 1985. *The Slave's Narrative*. New York: Oxford University Press.

Gluck, Barbara Reich. 1979. *Beckett and Joyce: Friendship and Fiction*. Lewisburg, Pa.: Bucknell University Press.

Humphrey, Robert. 1954. *Stream of Consciousness in the Modern Novel*. Berkeley: University of California Press.

Marcus, James. 1986. "The Pain of Being Two." Review of *A Glance Away*,

Hurry Home, The Lynchers, and *The Homewood Trilogy,* by John Edgar Wideman. *Nation,* October 4, pp. 321–22.

O'Brien, John, ed. 1973. *Interviews with Black Writers.* New York: Liveright.

Plummer, William. 1985. "John Edgar Wideman." *People Weekly,* February 11, pp. 121–22, 124, 127–28, 131.

Samuels, Wilfred. 1983. *"Going Home:* A Conversation with John Edgar Wideman." *Callaloo,* February, pp. 40–59.

Stepto, Robert B. 1979. *From behind the Veil: A Study of Afro-American Narrative.* Chicago: University of Illinois Press.

Thompson, Robert Farris. 1983. *Flash of the Spirit: African and Afro-American Art and Philosophy.* New York: Random House.

Wallace, Michelle. *Black Macho and the Myth of the Superwoman.* New York: Warner Books, 1980.

Werner, Craig. 1982. *Paradoxical Resolutions: American Fiction since James Joyce.* Urbana: University of Illinois Press.

Wideman, John Edgar. 1967. *A Glance Away.* Chatham: Chatham Bookseller.

———. 1970. *Hurry Home.* New York: Harcourt.

———. 1973. *The Lynchers.* New York: Dell.

———. 1977. "Defining the Black Voice in Fiction." *Black American Literature Forum* 11:79–82.

———. 1978a. *"Of Love and Dust:* A Reconsideration." *Callaloo* 1:76–84.

———. 1978b. "Stomping the Blues: Ritual in Black Music and Speech." *American Poetry Review* 7:42–45.

———. 1981a. *Damballah.* New York: Avon Books.

———. 1981b. *Hiding Place.* New York: Avon Books.

———. 1983. *Sent for You Yesterday.* New York: Avon Books.

———. 1984. *Brothers and Keepers.* New York: Holt Rinehart.

———. 1987. *Reuben.* New York: Henry Holt.

Index